THE MUSICIAN AND THE MICRO

Ray Hammond

BLANDFORD PRESS

Poole   Dorset

First published in the U.K. 1983 by Blandford Press,
Link House, West Street, Poole, Dorset, BH15 1LL

Copyright © 1983 Anderworth Ltd

British Library Cataloguing in Publication Data

Hammond, Ray
  The musician and the micro.
  1. Music—Data processing   2. Microprocessors
  I. Title
  001.64′04   ML63

ISBN 0 7137 1298 8 (Hardback)
ISBN 0 7137 1299 6 (Paperback)

The manuscript was originally written using a 'Scripsit' word-processing program on a Tandy
Model II microcomputer. The manuscript was edited at Blandford Press and corrections made
by the author to the electronically stored information held in the Scripsit program. The
keystrokes were electronically transferred to an an APS5 computer-controlled photo-
typesetting machine.

Jacket photograph of the Fairlight Computer Musical Instrument by Brian McMahon.

This book was typeset by Sprint Computerised Typesetting from keystroke information
supplied by Ray Hammond.

Printed in Great Britain by Butler & Tanner Ltd, Frome and London

Contents

Acknowledgements 4

Introduction 5

1 The Micro Concept 7

2 The Personal Micro and Music 22

3 The Micro in the Studio 38

4 The Micro as Teacher 51

5 The Micro and the Percussionist 72

6 The Micro in Performance 90

7 The Micro/Instrument Hybrids 104

8 The Micro in Sequence 115

9 The Mighty Micro: Dedicated Music Computers 124

10 The Micro and the Musician 147

Glossary of Jargon 176

Index 191

Acknowledgements

Acknowledgements: Thanks are due to the many individuals, companies, magazines and publishers who have willingly offered both time and expert advice in the preparation of this book. Of particular help were:

Apple Computers, Warren Cann, Richard Desmond, Peter Gabriel, Dave Green, Ikatro Kakehashi, Michael Kelly, John Lewis, Fred Mead, Tony Mitchell, Brian Nunney, Stephen Paine, John Pawsey, Philips Electrical, Tom Piggot, the Roland Companies in the UK and the USA, Martin Rushent, Kim Ryrie, Bill Stephen, Syco Systems Ltd, the Tandy Corporation, Cherry Watret and Hans Zimmer.

Special thanks are due to my wife, Elizabeth Hammond, who proof read this manuscript several times.

This book is for Jane, a musician of the future who will only have to be able to 'hear,' to play.

Introduction

This book is about the future of music. It assumes that the reader knows something about music but little about computers.

With the aid of computers, music has taken a sudden evolutionary jump and many musicians have stumbled at the fence. For some adults, computers and the high-tec jargon that surrounds them, represent one of the least attractive aspects of life in the late twentieth century. Artists especially are dismissive of such coldly calculating objects, preferring to place their belief in human inspiration and instinctive creativity.

But the computer has become a friendly beast. It is here to offer assistance with life's problems and despite the difficulties that will undoubtedly occur as it arrives in society, in the long term it promises to help man fulfil himself.

Music is in all of us, to a greater or lesser extent, but for many enthusiastic fans, expression is locked away inside, unable to get out because the body lacks a means of physical expression.

Life has so much to offer, that time may not be available to train the body to express itself musically. Until now it has been necessary to school fingers, lips and feet to perform unnatural tasks for music production. such training often spans years before music-making becomes natural enough for melody to flow unimpeded from the mind to the outside world.

Now the computer liberates the music in all of us. There is no longer the need for years of piano practice, agonized months of violin scrapings and the deliberate cultivation of finger-tip callouses. The computer will take over the mechanical parts of the job, and allow us to make melody, to sing, allowing the music to pour forth.

Such statements seem shocking (if not nonsensical) when applied to the ritually formal and stylized world of classical music, but here, as in all other music spheres, computers have much to offer and no power to harm.

Some long-held attitudes will change as a result of this revolution. Technically-proficient musicians have long been held in high regard, but if their skill can be equalled, or exceeded, by a computer their future as the mechanical reproducers of music must be limited. Of course, the greatest performers, those who breathe originality into each performance, will remain inviolate, their skills even more clearly defined by their very humanity.

This book is, of necessity, only an introduction to the subject of computer aid for music making. Interested readers are urged to get 'hands on' experience as further instruction is hard to contemplate unless it is accompanied by practical experience.

The computer is an ally, helping Man make better music.

Ray Hammond,
Bath,England
January 1983

1 The Micro Concept

'The guitar will be gone
within ten years — Microchips!'
Pete Townshend.*

Peter Gabriel composes and creates most of his music using a computer. So do Ultravox, Kraftwerk, Stevie Wonder, The Human League, Orchestral Manoeuvres in the Dark, Neil Young, Jean-Michel Jarre, Toto, Landscape, Tangerine Dream, Keith Emerson and a growing army of successful musicians and composers. Why?

Gabriel: 'I have no technique really, no training, no formal understanding whatever — as is true for a lot of rock people. But now I am able to do things which before would have had to incorporate professional, specially trained musicians.'

Warren Cann (Ultravox): 'It took me about a month to get used to machine tempo and then I started really getting off on it. I used to think: "it's not really me against the machine."'

The computer offers great power over music, compressing into weeks, tasks that would otherwise take months and freeing musicians to concentrate on the quality of their music rather than on its mechanical production.

In this book, and in the music business generally, you will see and hear the terms 'micro', 'computer', 'microprocessor' and 'chip' used interchangeably; it might be a good idea to clear up any confusion early on although a Glossary of Jargon appears at the back of this book. In most cases the four terms mean precisely the same thing. Jargon is the curse of the computer age. Computing is a new science and whilst every science has its own language, computers will be used by everybody, not just scientists, and jargon is a barrier to understanding.

A microprocessor is a small group of electronic circuits laid on top of each other on one silicon chip. They are usually cased in rectangular black-plastic housings about .5 in. (13mm) long x .25 in. (6.5mm). Half-a-dozen metal 'legs' protrude from both long sides and they are usually fixed to a printed circuit board by these legs (which also serve as the electrical connectors). The circuit itself is very much smaller than the black-plastic case and the only reason that the casing

* Rolling Stone, June 24th, 1982.

7

is so large is to allow humans to handle the tiny circuits. There is one more important feature about microprocessors: they are CHEAP, and they are getting still cheaper. A chip that was $5.38 in February 1980 costs $1 as this book goes to press. It is this combination of power and low cost that is the key to the revolution which is overtaking music (and almost every other aspect of our lives).

The circuits in the chip combine to form the processing unit of a computer – a machine that is capable of being programmed to carry out tasks of logic. You must alter your understanding of the word 'computer' in order to understand this revolution properly. Where the definition formerly read: 'a room full of equipment smothered in knobs and dials with vertical open-reel tapes spinning endlessly' it must now read: 'a minute group of circuits that may be programmed to carry out logical tasks.'

It isn't necessary for any musician to understand the details of how a computer works, but the first hurdle is to accept that a tiny circuit, such as the one we're describing, can be a *complete computer*. All that is required is a method for us to communicate with it and a method for it to communicate with us.

Only a few years ago a room full of equipment would have been needed to produce the computing power contained in today's average $5 production chip. The enormous increase in computer power stems from the stunning technological developments of the last 30 years and it is important to realize that this development is still continuing and *increasing* in speed. Thus in five years we are likely to find one tiny chip that is a hundred times more powerful than production chips today.

By now it must have become obvious that the term power is used a great deal when describing computers. Power means the speed at which a computer works and its amount of memory.

The tiny computer in the chip, the microprocessor, often consists of three separate circuits, although these circuits are sometimes separated on different chips. The three circuits are usually an ALU (arithmetic/logic unit), a control-logic unit and a control-memory unit. It is memory capacity which transforms the chips into computers because the ability to remember is the ability to learn, and so we encounter our first concept of artificial intelligence. The arithmetic/logic unit carries out the addition and subtraction of numbers necessary in a program and also makes comparisons for logical reasons. The control unit is precisely what it sounds, a circuit for

8

controlling what the arithmetic/logic and memory circuits are doing whilst 'interfacing' (connecting) them to the outside world (you).

Every computer in the world remembers things by numbers, but only the two digits 1 and 0 are used in an endless variety of combinations (e.g.10111000). This method of counting is called the binary code. Computers seem more friendly, more human perhaps, when it is realized that the things can't multiply or divide as we do. If a computer has to divide 1,000 by 12, the computer adds up twelves until 1,000 is exceeded, takes one off, calculates the decimal fraction left over and delivers the complete answer. This trial and error process of carrying out mathematical functions is effective only because it is done so quickly.

Even computers which remember music or words actually store their memories as numbers, converting their memories into sounds or words when commanded to do so and returning them to memory as numbers when they are not required. Typically a computer will use

Jean-Michel Jarre, the French composer and performer, pictured here during his pioneering tour of the Chinese Republic during 1981. He transported his Fairlight Computer Musical Instrument and several tons of equipment from gig to gig coping with small problems, such as discovering only one power socket available, as he went.

a long string of numbers to record one tiny element of a sound, perhaps 10111000. Thousands or millions of these strings of numbers called 'bytes' will be needed to make up one sequence of sounds, each string having to be read, interpreted and produced on cue and at a rate well beyond human abilities, perhaps even beyond real human comprehension. The average chip is capable of 'reading' perhaps 100,000 such strings in one hundreth of a second! So when we talk about power we are really talking about the amount of information we can get a chip to remember and store. You would be entitled to feel that the absurdly fast calculations a micro can make are sufficient for most tasks, but as the speed increases so can the complexity and the number of strings stored, and thus the accuracy of reproduction (of sound for example) improves.

The present generation of chip-computers is just capable of creating musical sounds that are perfect to our ear but as we demand our thinking machines to become more and more intelligent, so the speed requirement increases.

The Ultra Intelligent Machine — the UIM to jargon freaks — which is promised to equal or exceed human intelligence by the turn of the century, will have to be able to carry out a thousand tasks at once — seeing, hearing, talking, calculating, sensing, considering — before it passes the test as being a machine with human or super-human capability. But technology does not seem to be a barrier. The Josephson Junction, a device invented in the 1960s by a British physicist, is enabling researchers to develop microprocessor circuits which operate at a speed that threatens to approach the ultimate barrier, the speed of light. The technique involves cooling ordinary conductors until they become 'super-conductive' and although these devices are at present still confined to laboratories, the enormous power they offer will soon be commercially available.

Examining how a computer uses numbers to store a sound is a task that is exhausting and is probably best left to the designers and programmers of 'digital' musical instruments. I have deliberately used the term digital because it seems to be the description most favoured by the manufacturers of computer-aided musical instruments. Some marketing men worry that the term computer or microprocessor, when applied to their instruments, will scare off potential buyers so they opt for digital, a term that has become acceptable in the music business because digital delays and other devices have been available for some years and the term has an acceptability factor that computer has not.

Many musicians over 20 have only the vaguest notion of what a digital instrument or sound processor is although younger players may well have achieved some *computer literacy* at school or college. Many attempt to consider it in relationship to 'analog', a phrase that has become familiar because of the synthesizer.

Ikataro Kakehashi, the President of the Japanese Roland Corporation, one of the foremost producers of computer-assisted musical devices, even considers that musicians over 25 will find it difficult, if not impossible, to get to grips with computer instruments.

The analog synthesizer was popularized in the 1960s by Dr Robert Moog and because it produced a new, exciting range of music-like sounds which could be controlled by a conventional keyboard, it became a popular 'space-age' instrument. By today's standards, it is a crude music-making tool, although if a microprocessor is used to control an analog synthesizer, the instrument can take on far greater dimensions.

Analog means 'the same language' or 'similar to' (from analogous). That is not quite a dictionary definition, but it is a practical one. In the analog synthesizer the musician presses a note on the keyboard and an electrical contact sends a voltage to an oscillator. Depending on how that oscillator is set up, an electrical signal is produced which is similar in character to a sound wave. When amplified and fed to a loudspeaker a corresponding sound is produced. Modification of the oscillator and the addition of others, along with other signal-modifying circuits, make up the analog synthesizer. Although its name would appear to have developed because of the instrument's ability to mimic, the analog synthesizer is at its best when it produces its own oscillator voices rather than when it attempts to synthesize the sounds of conventional instruments.

It is analog because the electricity sent to the oscillator produces an electrical reaction and that electrical signal, analogous to a sound wave, is modified and amplified as an electrical signal before being turned into sound waves by the loudspeaker. Throughout the production of sound the signal remained an electrical voltage.

In digital circuitry the musician may still create an initial voltage when he depresses a note on a keyboard, but the circuitry (via an analog to digital converter) rapidly translates that electrical signal into a string of numbers (10111000) which are then held in the chip memory or retranslated back into an electrical voltage to feed a loudspeaker. So what's the advantage? If analog can produce sounds in one electrical form, what's to be gained by going through the two extra stages of translation, before and after the digital processor, to produce a sound? The answer is: EVERYTHING!

Firstly, the sound, or rather its corresponding numbers, can be remembered by the processor as long as there's power in the circuit. Secondly, because we're dealing with numbers, which represent each element of a sound — it's frequency, 'envelope shape', modulation, 'ADSR', tempo etc (see glossary at back) — and which can modify sound in any way we want to, it is under our complete control. Here is an example of a typical application:

You play a piece of music and it is recorded digitally. Every element of the sound is expressed as a number and held in a memory bank of numbers. After your performance you realised that you played it too slowly. Because it's recorded in numbers you only have to 'access' (find) the numbers which control the tempo, to re-write them to play more quickly. The pitch doesn't change because the numbers governing frequency can stay the same, so the singer can still sing in precisely the same key but the tempo can be doubled if necessary. Equally, you could alter the number strings which govern pitch but not speed; so a piece is instantly transposed to another key *after* recording, without altering the tempo. That is only the most minor of the tricks that become possible once the music is stored digitally. But by now you may be thinking that the only way you'll be able to use this technology is if you learn how to access specific strings of numbers and re-write them. This is true, but it isn't nearly as difficult as it sounds. Manufacturers of computer products for musicians understand that these must be easy for musicians to use (computer people call it 'user-friendly') and so, if you wish to increase the tempo without changing pitch, they provide a button marked tempo! Just using this button allows you to access the number strings controlling tempo so you really don't have to learn the long string of 11011010 or anything like it. Similarly a transpose switch will access all the number strings controlling pitch and alter them according to your new setting.

Instruments that are more computer-based, general-purpose computers rather than musical instruments, will require you to define the area you want to alter — pitch, tempo, etc — but control of these parameters is only marginally harder than on the dedicated (one purpose only) machines specially made for musicians.

The Human League are one of the best-known 'computer bands'. With their producer, Martin Rushent, they work out each bar of a song before recording and key the music into a Roland MC-8 MicroComposer. 'Effects', such as acoustic drums, are added later.

Digital recording holds the sound (or 'information' as it should properly be called) in a microprocessor memory. We've already seen how tempo or pitch may be altered; the same applies to every other element of the sound. A digital instrument may have many micro-processors contained in its circuitry and its memory capacity may be vast. Instruments are now on the market which will 'record' 16 'channels' of recording at once, with a typical maximum piece length of between five and sixty minutes, depending on system. This allows the musician to play 16 polyphonic parts and then replay them in perfect synchronization – rather like having a 16-track tape machine built into the keyboard.

Because any part of the sound(s) may be altered, the musician, realizing that a particular chord should have been a minor instead of a major, has only to access (find and recover) the offending note's string of numbers in the memory store and alter it to the right string. The practical way of doing this is to use an edit mode. The machine plays back the contents of one or all of its memories – at a slower tempo than performance tempo if desired – and at the appropriate place the musician plays the minor chord he should have played the first time. Bingo! The recording now has the minor chord where the major was. This simple technique applies to individual notes, chords, specific sounds and every element of sound. Thus he can compose and change, editing endlessly, altering the speed, the key, the sounds themselves at will. But he may have programmed the keyboard to produce different sounds on each of the 16 'tracks,' or indeed have changed sounds while working on one track — he can go as slowly as he wishes, building and editing individual tracks. I am not describing an instrument of the future, they are here now, commercially available and relatively inexpensive.

You will have noticed some familiar terms in that description of a keyboard. 'Channel,' for example, allows musicians to relate to the independent channels in mixing boards or amplifiers. 'Tracks' is used, referring to multi-track tape recording, but these terms, which musical product manufacturers seem to have retained in describing computer-based instruments, should be considered as merely an aid to visualization, not a literal description.

By now the musician must be asking; 'But what *sound* will I be making when I press these keys?' I mention keys only because keyboards are currently the most popular and convenient control-and-input method. The technology will work perfectly well with other inputs but little development has yet taken place to allow fretted or wind instruments to provide direct input. After the musical keyboard the typewriter-style alphanumeric keyboard is the second most popular method of supplying input and it is likely that voice control will shortly become inexpensive and popular.

At present the most successful digital instruments have pre-set sounds that have been recorded and stored by digital means. The musician still reaps the benefit of true sound reproduction — if it's supposed to be a clarinet it will sound *precisely* like a clarinet — speed and transposition control, editing and so on, but he is limited to the sounds provided by the manufacturer. But hold on! The central computing unit in the instrument may be programmed to produce any sound at all — a pack of dogs barking if you like! So most manufacturers have devised a way of loading sounds (programs) into the instrument. This may be achieved in a variety of ways, but almost without exception the storage medium for these programs is a magnetic tape or disk or similar device.

Digital Keyboards, Inc. of New York provide cartridges with their

Synergy digital keyboard. The cartridges store programs on a magnetic material and each cartridge offers the player 24 sounds. When the performer slots in a cartridge he can select any of the 24 sounds – one cartridge might offer traditional instrument sounds, trumpet, violin, oboe etc, another cartridge, electronic sounds, and so on – and during performance he can switch between sounds and between cartridges, loading and re-loading the program sounds at will.

E-mu Systems, Inc. of Santa Cruz, California offer their Emulator with a disk which slots into the front panel and loads particular sounds. These 'floppy disks,' rather like a give-away record but housed in a paper sleeve, are a popular way of storing information on small computers. The E-mu system allows the musician to record on to the disk and thus off-load complete recordings on to the disks to be recalled later (see Chapter 7). Both companies offer the service of transferring any customer's own sounds (produced with tin lids if you like) on to their magnetic storage mediums for use with their keyboards.

There are many other manufacturers producing similarly programm-able but pre-set keyboards, and my mention here of these two does not offer any particular endorsement save that I have worked with both and know them to function well. Other systems operate in different ways and in this early phase of the musical application of the microprocessor, manufacturers are clearly developing individual storage and program-loading systems to ensure that their own sounds can't be copied and used elsewhere and also to ensure a loyalty to their brand as new and better instruments become available.

The problem of the copyright of software (programs) is a difficult one. It is something that is absorbing the entire computer industry. In an ideal world all machines using computer technology, including musical instruments, would be compatible. For example, if every manufacturer agreed that the best magnetic storage medium was a paper-sleeved disk, or a 'bubble memory,' the one principle might be adopted for everything. By the very nature of programs, whether designed to produce a musical sound or to navigate a space-shuttle, they must be accessible, i.e. you must be able to transfer the particular string of digits that constitute a program into the live part of the computer, the bit that does the work.

The heart of the computer is called the CPU (central processing unit) and the live memory I mentioned is called RAM (random access memory). It is a lot of jargon, but RAM is an excellent way to describe a circuit of microscopic transistors joined together in such a way that they remember which ever number they are asked to (1 or 0) and allow the user to find out instantly what they remember no matter where they are in the circuit.

Because all programs can be easily off-loaded it follows that they are relatively easy to copy. Some can be partially protected with passwords or codes, although any knowledgeable programmer can seemingly undo any other knowledgeable programmer's protection. For example, on a computer-assisted musical instrument which uses floppy disks for storing and loading sounds, one owner can loan his programs to another for the evening and with the addition of a little programming knowhow and a second instrument, or a system for using the disk known as a disk drive, the second owner can copy all the sound programs his friend has bought. That might not sound too serious, but no complex program is quick to create, and many take months or years to perfect. Consequently many manufacturers are preparing their software in ways which prevent illegal copying — except at tremendous difficulty and cost.

The programmers are finding themselves in a similar position to that faced by music publishers and composers versus the photo-copy machine. It has long been a complaint that bandleaders buy one complete score for a tune, photocopy it and distribute it to the band, thus saving the purchase of 30 copies. Composers and music publishers have long given up fighting that one, but in some countries writers are still fighting lending libraries, record companies are still fighting the blank cassette tape, film companies are worried about illegal video-tape copying and so on. But logic would appear to suggest that there is now no protection for any single published piece of creation which is stored electronically and total reward must be sought before publication.

The instruments I describe above are only half-way houses. They are designed for musicians who have learned their skills on traditional instruments and would find a fundamental change in their thinking very difficult to make. Within a few years, however, the children now at school, programming computers with ease, will be the young, professional musicians of tomorrow and they will regard such pre-set parameters as unacceptable, rather as we now view the early analog synthesizers. In ten years, most music will start in the mind, and the computer, which is getting cheaper and more powerful all the time, will create what we hear. It will still be human music because it comes from human inspiration, but there's a new means of translating thought into action.

It would be wrong to regard computer-aided music as artificial. Every traditional instrument, the piano, the violin, is an artificial machine built by man to create a pleasing sound and allow the production of that special combination of sounds we call music. The computer is no more artificial than a Steinway grand.

What really is profound in this revolution is the shift in emphasis that will follow: A SHIFT FROM THE PERFORMER TO THE COMPOSER!

Our society has revered both the performer and the composer for different skills. The performer can, on almost any given occasion, use physical skills gained by long practice to produce live music. The quality of the music depends on the abilities of the performer and if he's playing music written by a great composer, the gifted performer can create a deeply emotional experience for himself and for his audience. But the composer has had no control over that performance of his work, or any other, beyond the notes and comments contained within the score. In the hands of a mediocre performer – or even a great one with a headache – even the greatest score can sound awful. It is the performer who makes all the decisions in a live performance. Just to keep you up to date with the jargon, computer people would describe a live performance as being in 'real-time' (i.e.happening now), to differentiate it from music which has been created at an earlier time, stored digitally and is now being recreated on demand – almost like playing back a recording, but not quite. The actual sounds are recreated over again each time, rather than a recording of an earlier performance being replayed.

This shift in emphasis will have a profound effect on performances. Many performer/composers are now choosing to create most of their music prior to the point of performance – whether for a live human audience or in a recording studio makes little difference – perhaps adding only one line, or colour to the piece, or pieces during performance. What they are doing is shifting the creation of the music out of real-time and into a time domain which gives them more control. They may choose to spend a day building up one ten second sequence of notes, with between three or four simultaneous sounds. Obviously that degree of perfection could never be contem-

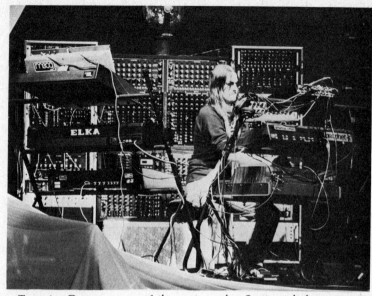

Tangerine Dream are one of the most popular Continental electronic-music groups. Kraftwerk are better known for their 'robot' music, but Tangerine Dream incorporate the computer and use it as a tool to create sounds rather than taking a style from the technology itself.

plated in a live (real-time) performance. The audience is listening to our performer/composer unveil a work he may have taken months to create. He may, or may not, choose to play an instrument live as his music is recreated. At one end of the scale all of the music except a background sequence of notes may be in real-time with the band bashing away remembering only to synchronize themselves with the 'sequencer' when necessary. The logical extension of this picture is of a composer walking on to a stage where his array of computers and amplification is set up. He might draw a chair to the centre of the stage, start the computer program running and let his composition sweep into the auditorium, only moving 45 minutes later to take his bow for a composition on which he has spent thousands of hours. Why bother? Why not keep all that information in a digital form, perhaps on a disk a few inches round, and distribute it to his audience's homes where they can replay it digitally — and thus perfectly – enabling them to *re-create* the music he has written? Good question. Clearly the nature of performance will change.

It is also possible that the advent of computer control over music will finally make real-time musical skills even more valued than they are today. Perhaps after a decade of listening to finely sculpted music created out of real-time, we will again clamour to hear the pianist with the best combination of expression and technique play person-ally for us – live. The one element which would be self-defeating to recreate by computer would be the human voice and vocalists may well gain an even greater stature in the performing arts.

Now the composer can sit with his computer and create in isolation, with the knowledge that he is also his own performer. By tradition, the genius composer sits before a blank sheet of manuscript paper and 'hears' precisely how a group of notes and instruments will sound. He writes this down using traditional music notation of treble and bass staves and, when performed, they sound precisely as he originally heard them — at least, that's the traditionalist's view. In fact, the evidence is that only a very few composers have ever been that gifted. Most seem to have a fair idea of what a chord will sound like when played by certain sections of the orchestra but most have to sit before an instrument – usually a piano – and make sure that the notes work together as they imagine. The computer has brought an explosion to their world. No longer do they sit before manuscript paper, they sit before a screen on which the program has commanded empty staves to be drawn. How they write the notation on to the staves is up to them. If they're conservative they may type into the computer, 'Place a quarter note (crotchet) at Middle C on Staff 1.' If they're a little looser they may prefer to use their chosen instrument to create notes. This is connected to the computer and when they press a middle C and hold it for a chosen time, that note, in its correct time shape (quarter note, half note etc) appears on the stave. Clearly they can play endless runs and chords and the notes will just pour onto the staff or staves. All that is required to make this happen is the right 'interface' (connection) to make the computer understand the instrument, whether it's a keyboard, drum, or other input device. So almost all composers will soon choose to play what they create into a computer and watch the notes appear by magic on the staves on their television screens. Or will they? This facility opens up a far larger possibility. Today's composers can all play instruments to a greater or lesser extent, but not all players can compose. An interesting thought is that perhaps there are composers who can't play. Many people with a good 'ear' can invent melodies and in the past, other than singing into tape recorders, they have had no way of expressing themselves. It can be argued that those gifted with great melodic invention will almost certainly master an instrument, *because* the desire to express themselves melodically is so great. I am not convinced. We are all the products of our backgrounds as well as of our genetic make up, and these backgrounds may or may not have included musical opportunity. Provide our imaginary, non-playing, non-singing, composer with a small personal computer costing a few hundred dollars (or pounds) and a music-writing program and we may all benefit from his or her unleashed musical creativity. The

A microprocessor. This is the Texas TMS 9900, the chip used in the TI-499/A home computer.

musical language, notes, half notes, quarter notes, scales, keys, etc, is easy to learn. Easy, that is, compared with mastering a musical instrument. An averagely intelligent young person might be expected to learn the language in a few weeks given the right motivation; and the facility a computer offers certainly provides that!

Once musically literate, the non-playing composer can write any note he chooses on the screen staff. Having written a sequence he asks the computer to replay what he's written. Remember, on a reasonably-advanced unit he can alter the tempo, the pitch and the sound (clarinet, electric guitar, bagpipes) at will. So with a little dedication the non-player can write music and hear it played back to him. This facility is available now. Remember Casio's $70 VL-Tone introduced during the summer of 1981? That is precisely what it did with a limited range of sounds, using a LCD (liquid crystal display) instead of the screen. Devices are already under development which will free our unskilled composer, even from the need to understand conventional musical notation. A speech analyzer will allow him to sing in the notes he wants – nobody's embarrassed about singing to a machine – and then he can play it back as a tuba, a piano and, before long, a totally realistic human voice – he may choose one with a much better timbre than his own. Obviously those who can hear well but can't pitch their voice – and there are many – will still have to rely on other forms of input.

But it is not just non-musicians who will be drawn to inputting via non-musical devices. John Lewis, the Canadian-born, classically trained composer who runs the Electrophon Company in London has now virtually abandoned the use of a musical instrument in favour of a typewriter-style keyboard to create his music. He is writing and recording complex music for films and commercials, as well as creating his own original music, and he now finds composition easier and faster with an alphanumeric keyboard. (See Chapter 10).

Perhaps the single most important result of this revolution is the freeing of the individual from the need to master a particular musical instrument before he can make music! Now, if you can hear it, you can play it!

21

2 The Personal Micro and Music

At the end of 1981 home computers were in 500,000 homes across the USA. By the end of 1982 that figure had risen to 1.5 million. A similarly sustained future growth curve would put computers in every home by the end of 1986. Of course, that won't quite happen, but as prices continue to drop, a high rate of growth will be sustained and the home computer will be as common as the TV set by the end of the decade.

All of these computers are capable of controlling electronic musical instruments, *if* the right interface hardware and software is available – even the tiny Sinclair ZX81 which is currently the cheapest proper personal computer available.

The larger home computers, Apples etc, have sufficient power to become complex musical instruments capable of satisfying the most demanding professional musician. As a result, a wide range of software-based instruments is becoming available as add-on units for home computers.

The argument for selecting a soft instrument is pretty convincing. In the last ten years electronic musical instruments have become obsolescent very quickly as manufacturers produced better instruments each year. The soft instrument will have longer staying power as additions and improvements can be contained in uprated software which extracts more from the existing hardware.

Even soft instruments will, of course, require complete replacement as better hardware makes better software possible, but a computer-based instrument system established now is likely to have a valuable currency for at least five years despite the rapidity with which the micro revolution is developing.

Musicians who already have small home computers may use them to control music. As yet, there is no commercial interface system which allows units such as the Sinclair, Pet or TRS-80 to provide control over digital or analog synthesizers or recording consoles. But the methods of achieving such control exist, have been tested and are likely to become commercially available within the next few years. A computer costing a couple of hundred dollars can now store music created out of real-time, store it as a sequence and recall it at will.

Several 'bolt on' music packages exist for home computers and some of these will be described later in this chapter, but even the smallest computer can create sound.

For most musicians, the term 'oscillator' conjures up images of analog synthesizers. In computers, an oscillator is not necessarily a physical component, an oscillator can be built by software programming. A tone equal to A at 440 cycles per second is produced if the computer sends a current to a loudspeaker which it turns on and off 440 times per second. The speaker cone moves in sympathy with this oscillating current and the tone is produced. The sound wave produced will be a squarewave, of limited used in music making. But computer programs can be written which will provide instructions to make a series of notes at different frequencies just by altering the speed at which the computer switches the current on and off. Tones can be introduced by writing programs which slightly alter the length of intermediate oscillation and thus, in its simplest form, the computer can make music.

Writing 'interrupt' programs of this sort is wasteful in computer time, and many makers of musical packages for microcomputers prefer to supply hardware which will produce the tones and leave the microprocessor free to control sound production. These items of hardware are real digital oscillators and they are special chips with built-in timers which send the on-off signals at varying speeds under the control of the computer's processor.

A good starting place to examine how the personal computer can assist in music-making is with the cheapest computer on the British and USA markets – the Sinclair ZX81.

The excellent British magazine *Electronics and Music Maker* promoted the concept of adapting small computers to musical application in 1981/82 when they published a series called *Micromusic* in which the application of small computers to music making was explained. Some computing knowledge was required of readers and the magazine confidently reproduced the jargon of the industry as its main language. The first computer covered in the series was the Sinclair ZX81.

Clive Sinclair's outstanding contribution to the cause of mass computer literacy started in Britain and, as over 750,000 Sinclairs have been sold world-wide, the magazine could confidently run an extended series of articles concerning his superb product.

Unfortunately the limitations of the ZX81 demand that the musician who attempts to apply it to music control should have more than a passing acquaintance with computer languages. Indeed a working knowledge of ZX81 BASIC and the machine code on which the computer's main Z80 chip operates is a prerequisite. For musicians with more time than money and with a willingness to learn, these skills can be acquired relatively quickly – a couple of months perhaps. The ZX81 manual covers BASIC and many books are now available on the subject of the Z80 machine code.

As the ZX81 has no sound production components, such as a digital oscillator, there is little point in programming it to produce tones as an inflexible monophonic square wave is of little use to an experienced musician. The most useful application for this tiny computer is for the storage of information which will cause external synthesizers to play under its control. For any degree of power, it is necessary to add the 16K option RAM pack to the basic ZX81.

The computer is not fitted with input/output ports and these must be made up by the user. Electronics & Music Maker have published a circuit diagram for such a board with a full explanation of how to build and fit it to a ZX81. The easiest synthesizers to control with a modified Sinclair are those that use a digital encoding system, as instruments with control voltage input require an additional digital-to-analog converter (also covered by the magazine).

Interestingly two of the cheapest synthesizers on the market – the Wasp and the Gnat – may be driven by the Sinclair. These synths have been selling in Britain for under £200 and even with the expense of the Sinclair, the 16K Ram pack and the components to complete the interface, total cost of a computer-controlled, three-octave synthesizer (the Wasp finds another octave when used this way) is unlikely to be much over £300!

This ingenious system has limitations. Some notes are more difficult than others to achieve, and sustain isn't really possible. The system does have the ability to operate as a simple sequencer and the program Peter Maydew offers as an example in his *Electronics and Music Maker* series of articles has no editing facilities but is capable of polyphony.

A circuit for a DAC which allows the ZX81 to interface with a 'one volt per octave' analog synth is provided in the series of articles. The control program for the sequencer developed is written in machine code and is capable of driving up to seven synthesizers at once (with some additions to the hardware interface).

The concept in this sequencer program is to divide the music into equal events, the shortest being equal to the shortest note in the piece to be played — a 16th note (semi-quaver) for example. In this code a quarter note would occupy four events, a half note eight events and so on. The program allows the sequence to be synchronized to a drum machine or click track.

In use, the program allows the musician to write music for up to seven output voices and utilizing all seven the system is capable of storing 1,825 events (notes, rests and ancillary control instructions) per voice. Full facilities for dumping the stored sequence on the tape are provided.

The end product of this construction project is a 12,000 note sequencer which costs very little money. The effort required during the writing of the music is considerable, but for those musicians with a deep interest in computing (and there is a growing army of them) the end result is an achievement which points the way to the future when tiny, inexpensive systems will be commercially available to help us make our music. For the moment, non-technical musicians will have to be content with the bolt-on systems available — described later in this chapter.

A very much easier home computer to program for music-making is the Sharp MZ-80K. Although several times the cost of the Sinclair ZX81, the Sharp configuration allows musical notes to be programmed in both machine code and the easier BASIC programming language.

In BASIC the musician needs only to write commands for note values such as pitch and time for them to be replayed over the computer's internal speaker. Writing a musical sequence requires some knowledge of BASIC programming, but this is not a complex procedure. Notes over a three octave range will play at seven different tempos. Delving into the machine code of the Sharp leads to greater control over the music-making capabilities and with only a relatively small amount of programming the Sharp can be converted into a mini-dedicated music computer with full tuition facilities. Two other computer languages, Pascal and FORTH, are available for the Sharp and these are also capable of programming the computer's sound generating facility. They are both faster languages than BASIC.

Some sound generation boards are available for other popular micro-computers. All of these systems may be programmed to write music, but at the time of writing, nearly all them demand a degree of computing skill from the user. Musicians who are interested will find many music projects gracing the pages of the specialist computer magazines.

For musicians without programming ability there are several bolt-on music-making systems available for use with a variety of small computers. I have gathered together the simple programs produced by the mass manufacturers in Chapter 4, *The Micro as Teacher*, but the systems described here all have the ability to make music that would satisfy a serious musician.

The bolt-on systems fall into two groups; those that offer real-time playing capability and those that have to be programmed to play music. Two sub groups divide these into systems which use computer power to control analog sound production and systems that enable the computer to produce sound digitally (computer-generated wave-forms). Both systems have their own advantages at the moment, although it is likely that, as small chips become faster, the wholly digital types of sound production system will become the norm.

The ALF music system, made in Denver, Colorado, is concerned with harnessing computer power for non-real-time composition. At the heart of the ALF system are sound-generating boards which plug straight into spare circuit-card slots within the Apple providing the computer with up to nine sound voices. The tones are produced from squarewave generators on the voice cards which are then submitted to the brains of the package, ALF's sophisticated software control.

There is no musical keyboard in the ALF package and the musician must write his music on to a staff shown on the screen. A menu offers a range of note symbols at the bottom of the screen – whole notes (semi-breves) through to sixteenth notes (demi-semi-quavers) – and using the Apple's game paddles, the composer places one cursor on the note symbol required and a second on the staff position required. This system of entering music becomes very rapid (much more rapid than the system for the less expensive Musicomp Program described in Chapter 4) and one line may be written very quickly. As the ALF system offers the composer the use of up to nine voices (depending on how many voice cards he has purchased) there must obviously be a way of displaying several voices at once. ALF have solved this problem by inventing a new graphic display which divides the screen horizontally into the number of voices in use. An electronic dot then moves across the screen horizontally in each

This ad caused a storm in America when it appeared a couple of years ago. The 'Guitarpple' was a joke, built to symbolize the musical power of the Apple computer when fitted with an 'Alf' music card. The 'ALF' is a powerful non-real-time tool, but even it can not support a guitar neck glued to an Apple. Bill Fickas, of Alf, who posed for the picture, has been denying the 'Guitarpple's' existence ever since. Photo courtesy of Alf Products Inc.

'channel' representing the movement of each note: low is to the left, high to the right. A central mark on the screen denotes middle C position and it is easy to see how the pitch of each voice is moving in relationship to its fellows.

The ALF system is cheap (a few hundred dollars per three voice board) and various software programs are available to control it. The 'Entry' program is the basic music-making package, 'Introduction' concerns basic musical and acoustic principles and 'Musical Skills' is a musical tuition program. It is fair to say that the professional applications for the ALF system are limited because of the lack of variation in the squarewaves on which the tones are produced, but it is an extremely powerful tool for a composer wishing to test out melody construction and arrangements.

For technologically-oriented musicians who are familiar with both sound and computer theory, there's a package for Commodore PET computers, and other computers with an 8-bit parallel output port, that is very interesting and quite inexpensive. Called the 'MTU Instrument Synthesis Package,' the program is entirely software based, demands no hardware modification to the computer for sound generation and only one board for DAC purposes. One of the program's authors is Hal Chamberlin, author of the superb book *Musical Application of Microprocessors* which is to be recommended to all readers who wish to learn about the techniques of applying microprocessors to music production. It was published by The Hayden Book Company of New Jersey in 1980. The price was $25. The MTU program, named after Hal Chamberlin's Micro Technology Unlimited company, builds sounds in purely digital form in a small-scale imitation of the dedicated music computers, like the Fairlight, (described in Chapter 9) and delivers it via a DAC. Package costs in Britain are under £100. The program is difficult to use, requiring the musician to write proper program lines. There are no menus and the user needs to understand the hexadecimal code in order to enter parameters for note pitch and duration. With time and patience, exciting sounds can be created by using the program's Fourier additive-synthesis techniques (also explained in Chapter 9). Limitations of the 8-bit DAC technology available with the PET and similar computers force the bandwidth to an upper limit around 3.5K but, despite this drawback, the program is cheap enough to entice all those capable of handling it. Be warned, however, the manual is written for those with full musical, acoustic and programming knowledge. At the time of writing, a new, friendlier version of the program was promised.

For under $1,000, Mountain Computer offer a music package for Apples which is probably the ultimate composition package available for home computers. It has no musical keyboard and thus cannot function as a real-time instrument. In all other respects it is a superb example of a computer instrument and a clear pointer to the very exciting musical aids to come.

The Mountain 'MusicSystem' consists of two hardware boards, two software disks and a manual. The printed-circuit boards slot directly into the bus bays in the Apple. Attached to one board is a 'light pen' which assists the user in programming from the screen.

The Mountain sound generation system is unique, although the company also supplies versions of the system which are incorporated into the Passport Soundchaser digital system and the Syntauri systems, both of which have the advantage of a real-time musical keyboard. There are 16 voices available in the Mountain system and the sounds are digitally created by the user. On creation, the 256K-byte waveform tables are transferred into the Apple's RAM and, during playback, the system uses the very rapid DMA (direct memory access) system to read the tables 500,000 times per second. The use of DMA is the key to the Mountain package and allows truly digital sound to be created in a small computer.

Each waveform generator on the MusicSystem boards has software loadable registers that contain the information on amplitude, wave-form table address (in RAM) and frequency. Other parts of the board have control over overall volume etc and these can be controlled by the composer from software.

As with most 8-bit systems, there is some background noise from the Mountain system which mars the otherwise superb sound. Upper end frequency response is 13Khz and although this isn't quite good enough for the very best professional applications, few musicians would be concerned.

The Mountain system offers considerable value for money and is a clear indication of the power the micro has to offer to music. The serious student or composer will find great potential in the system. Apart from the quality and flexibility of the digitally-produced voices, the 16 independent sounds which can play simultaneously open considerable compositional and arrangement possibilities.

In accordance with the software trend, the system is very user-friendly, being menu-driven throughout and leaving little room for misunderstanding. The manual that accompanies the system is excellent, although it must be read before running the program. Our consumerist habits of plugging in first and opening the manual later have got to change; the new technology demands greater respect. From the opening menu the user is led to other menus (in a software architecture known as 'nested menus'). If the user's selection requires further decisions to be made, the subsequent menus appear on the screen until all decisions have been made and the computer can execute the task. The software is tolerant of illegal commands and merely displays a prompt to that effect, returning to the previous menu for a re-selection. Most of the menus require only one keystroke and subsequent entry. If the computer undertakes a task that takes some time, the screen shows an explanation of what is going on.

The software package is divided into four main programs. The four functions are 'Music Player', 'Instrument Definer', 'Music Editor' and 'Music Merger.' In use the Music Editor program divides the screen with the upper part displaying the music staves and the lower part offering the menu selection. As an indication of the power of the Mountain program, it should be explained that the screen is a window on to the score in process and this score may be scrolled right or left to show the composer the section required and up and down to show each of the 16-parts. The staff formats available include treble, alto, bass and system clef and the user can change clef at any time.

The Editor program can operate in both a single note and chord mode. In the chord mode the composer adds notes to the chord without the display moving on. The light pen (or light sensitive pen as it should properly be called) is used to select the note required (sixteenth or quarter note for example) and the game paddle places the note on the desired position on the staff. Key signatures are set at the beginning of entry and all flats and sharps are automatically made when the corresponding note is entered.

From the Editor mode the music that has been entered may be printed via an Apple printer (not as a banked 16 part, but as individual staves which can be stuck together if necessary).

The Instrument Definer program allows the user to define all the parameters of the waveform − envelopes for all elements of sound − and create unique sounds. During the creation of sounds there is a constant audio playback which allows the user to hear the results of the envelopes being created. The parameters in the Instrument Definer program are individual volume for the voice, relative to the other voices in use, the attack profile, the frequency history (this allows the frequency to change inside the note, making such variations as vibrato possible) and sustain exponential. The waveform itself must also be defined from a menu.

In addition to defining envelopes for the above elements, a sub-program offers the choice of creating sound using additive synthesis – as in the dedicated music computers. This system allows the composer to build a sound by adding harmonic amplitudes with the computer using the Fourier formula to fill in the gaps. This program accepts 24 harmonic settings, with a graphic display similar to a row of mixer faders supplying visual indications of harmonic settings. The result of the efforts can be heard as the harmonics are adjusted and this allows a sound to be created by ear. It is possible to combine a number of the waveform generators to produce a sound which has a variety of differing characteristics.

All usual facilities such as saving-to-disk, replay and file creation are offered by the program and it must currently rate as one of the best value-for-money micro-computer music programs available for non-real-time composition.

Real-time facilities as well as composition power are provided in two 'Soundchaser' systems from Passport Designs of California.

Both systems, one creating sounds by analog means, the other digitally, are based on the ubiquitous Apple 11. In the analog version, the hardware supplied in the package consists of a custom-built musical keyboard and interface and analog voice cards which are fitted into the Apple bus. To complete the system Passport supply their software on floppy disks. Once the musician possesses the system, there are other Passport software packages available offering a music tuition system and a music print program. All Passport software is written in Applesoft, the latest Apple language. The Apple in use must be either an Apple 11 plus or have an Applesoft ROM card.

In the analog package, the user has a choice of purchasing one or two voice cards offering three or six voices. The basic operating software offers two envelope generators (with floating sustain) and two low frequency oscillators – allowing the musician the chance to modify waveform shapes. Parameters over which control is available

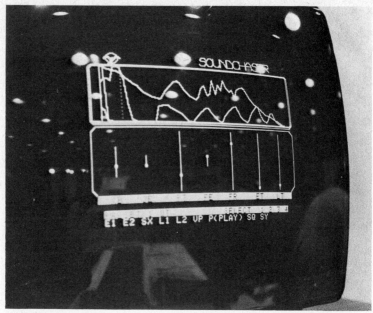

A waveform display from the 'Soundchaser' program produced by Passport Designs. This program runs on an Apple home computer and allows musicians to build sounds as well as to compose out of real-time.

include time value, loudness, resonance and frequency.

A built-in sequencer program allows the user to multi-track polyphonically, laying melodies over chords and adding bass lines at will. The sequencer has a capacity of over 3,000 notes which Passport claim allows storage of 10 to 15 minutes of music.

The digital system from Passport makes use of the sound production boards produced by Mountain Computers (described earlier). These digital oscillators produce eight voices and the software that accompanies this system allows the musician to define instruments by either drawing their waveforms on the screen or by specifying their harmonic content. Modifications to sounds created may be effected with the use of envelope generators, low frequency oscillators and effects generators.

The keyboard supplied by Passport is identical in both the analog and digital packages. It is a 49-note unit and the interface card which is fitted to the Apple 11 provides the 'keys down' information to the computer. On the analog voice card, each voice is created by the use of an oscillator, a wave shaper and filter and an amplifier — similar to a conventional analog synthesizer. A 24 dB/octave resonant wave low-pass filter completes the sound production chain.

On 'booting up' the Apple 11 with the Soundchaser disk the user is presented with a menu offering 'Help', 'Disk', 'Edit' or 'Seq(uence)'. The Help facility offers a help menu with operating guidelines. The Disk option is used when storing or retrieving work from disk, Edit is the main sub-program for playing, creating or altering sounds and the Seq function allows the user to create and play back sequences. In the Edit mode the user is presented with a two-part graphic display. The upper part of the screen is called the 'contour window' and in this the musician may draw curves which will define one element of the sound being created. The bottom half of the screen is described as the 'voice panel' and this consists of the graphic representation of three switches and four linear faders which allow the musician to define the other elements of the sound.

At the bottom of the screen a menu is displayed allowing the user to select from one of the four preset sounds supplied. Alternatively he may opt to create sounds. If P (for preset) is selected along with the appropriate choice of preset sound, the voice information is loaded and the player may play the musical keyboard as a real-time instrument.

If the player decides to shape his own sound he starts with a contour window. Four basic envelopes are set-up by the software. The first curve is for volume, or amplitude. This controls the loudness variation of the note through attack, decay, sustain and release. Each contour consists of 64 data points plotting the curve. On normal Apple displays the progress of the curve is shown by 'stars' but with the optional high-resolution Apple display the curve is drawn with considerably more detail. Using the game paddles fitted to most Apples, the user can move the cursor into the path of the curve, push the 'fire' button once and enter the Soundchaser plotting mode. In this mode the user may proceed to draw the curve of his choice. Pressing P for play allows the musician to hear the result of his curve experiment at any time. The second envelope controls modulation of the pitch of the note oscillator and/or the tuned frequency of the resonant low-pass filter during the ADSR (attack-decay-sustain-release) period of the sound's birth and death. The other two curves are for the two low-frequency oscillators, L1, modulating the frequency delivered by the LFO and L2, modulating the resonate frequency of the filter.

In the bottom half of the screen is the graphic representation of seven controls. The first of these selects which octave range the four-octave keyboard works on. A total range of seven octaves is available. Other controls turn envelopes on and off, and govern tuning, the time duration over which the envelope develops and tuning for the LFOs. Typing the key names for these controls places the cursor on them and the game paddle will move the controls as required. These methods of sound control are quite powerful and a wide range of sounds may be created. Returning to the Disk option on the operating menu allows the user to store the sound he has built. The operating software isn't foolproof and warnings abound in the manual advising users to avoid hitting the reset button during creation as this wipes RAM and destroys what ever has been created.

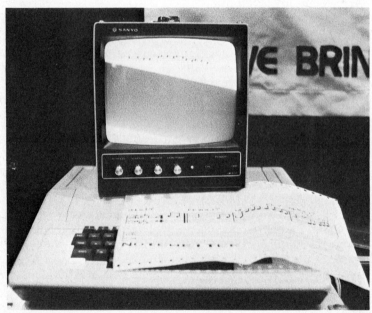

The 'Soundchaser' software allows composers to print 'hard copy' of their musical scores.

On the Apple the reset button is located rather perilously on the top right of the keyboard, not safely separated as on some computers, and this presents a real risk to lengthy compositions. Knowledgeable programmers can adapt a program to disable the re-set button but this produces its own difficulties.

Passport are justifiably proud of their sequencer program. All of the usual controls are provided; tempo, pitch, etc, with the tempo limit set at 16 times faster or slower than the original recording. The four sequencer memory banks have room for 128 notes or chords (256 events) each, and the program has overdub facilities which allow the musician to build up layered tracks. Only the keystroke information is stored in the sequencer program and all other parameters such as voice tones, envelopes and pitch may be varied on replay. During recording, a sequence in any of the four memory banks may be pre-assigned to use a particular 'patch' which is called 'preset' in the Soundchaser system. This corresponds to a complete set-up consisting of voice selection with all sound modifications made. During replay the sequence will automatically play the arrangement laid down for it. The first part of the sequence may play on voice one with a deep, rough pre-set, the second part of the sequence, from the second bank, may use a high, soaring sound and so on.

The real beauty of the Passport system is economy. Excluding the cost of the Apple, the package can be had for around $1,000.

alphaSyntauri are another new corporation producing a computer-based real-time musical instrument. Again they are based in California (the whole state should now change its name to 'Silicon Valley') and the package they produce is able to perform several functions. Their 'Music Teaching System' is described in Chapter 4, but their music making packages are serious instruments for the professional musician. This is reflected in a price range which spans the $1,000 to $3,000 market. On top of this cost a user has to find another few thousand dollars for a home computer, again the Apple 11.

The system packages are tailored to fit different needs and different budgets. At the top end the 'Studio Pro' system comprises a five octave, velocity-sensing keyboard (C-C), two foot expression pedals, interface hardware boards for connecting with the Apple and sound generation synthesizer boards. The system produces eight voices and also includes software which provides sequencer capacity alphaSyntauri describe as a 16-track recording system.

As the packages are scaled down for smaller budgets, the keyboard eventually shrinks to a four octave unit which is not velocity-sensitive and the software provided contains either a simplified sequencer or, in the cheapest version, no sequencer at all.

alphaSyntauri's marketing approach typifies the fragmented instrument-market musicians now face. This comment implies no disrespect to the company's marketing methods, rather it highlights the soft nature of computer-based products in which packages can be tailored for specific needs with only minimum hardware adjustment. In making the right choice, the musician requires a real knowledge of the options in front of him. Sadly, most musicians have not yet gained this knowledge and will either pay for facilities which are useless to them or will find themselves having to update the package after their initial purchase. Thankfully, the 'soft' nature of the concept allows such updating to be done at reasonable cost without discarding all the hardware concerned.

The sound production system used by alphaSyntauri again comes from the Mountain Computer company but the addition of the keyboard and the software harnesses this considerable sound production power to a real-time instrument.

When the velocity-sensitive keyboard has been selected as part of the package, the musician may enter music in this way rather than type it in, and the computer senses how rapidly the keys are pressed down and released. This enables the musician to enter the notes in their actual time values directly onto the staff. The speed in which a small computer/software system can deliver a note after a key is depressed is always the critical test and the alphaSyntauri/Apple combination can deliver in a few milliseconds – fast enough for almost every musical purpose.

The alphaSyntauri software offers all of the usual facilities, such as sound creation, editing of music already created – including tempo control – and storing for later recall.

Real-time controls include the footpedals for assignable functions such as glide and sustain and the Apple's game paddles may also be used for such functions as vibrato.

alphaSyntauri also offer users the option of adding a program called 'The Composer's Assistant.' This program enables musical scores to be printed on to paper via a variety of computer printers. The print-out does not exactly match traditional music printing, but the company claim it is capable of providing composers with printed notation very similar to multi-staff piano scores.

The 'Metatrak' software package, also available as additional software for alphaSyntauri systems sold without the facility, is a '16 track digital recorder.' This software is currently unique among small-computer based instruments in offering a 16 channel sequencer with separate access to each of the 16 channels and the ability to edit individual notes within each channelled sequence. For ease of visualization, alphaSyntauri describe the channels as tracks and the analogy with an analog multi-track deck is useful when describing the functions. This facility ought to make some of the dedicated systems manufacturers start thinking!

As with 16-track tape machines, each track may be accessed separately, but in this program tracks can be tied together (end to end) to form lengthy sequences in a way impossible with its analog counterpart. Individual volume control is available over each of the tracks, making mixing possible during playback and some editing − changing of timbre, etc − is available on individual tracks during replay. Individual notes or individual tracks may be accessed after recording to alter volume or expression (vibrato, etc). Speed control during replay is 1 to 800% of the original speed and, of course, the musician has the obvious advantage of building tracks without any sound degradation or increased background noise. (See description of Mountain system for note about signal-to-noise ratio).

In its basic form, the Metatrack system offers a capacity of storing up to 2,000 notes and this requires a 64K Apple. A software and hardware modification is available as an optional extra. This modification increases note storage to 20,000 notes − a figure alphaSyntauri claim will produce an orchestral piece of 30 to 60 minutes duration. The price of the basic Metatrack software ($250 at the time of writing) is proof of the benefit to be derived from soft systems based on microcomputers.

3 The Micro in the Studio

Recording studios have been using microprocessor aids for some years. They have had the necessary money and suitably friendly locations to offer.

Microprocessors first appeared in studios as purely passive aids – accurately controlling the speed of tape transports and creating digital echo – but since 1974 studios have been using computers creatively. However, the word digital had passed into studio parlance a few years before the interactive microprocessor arrived.

Echo/reverberation is one of the major tools used in a recording studio and the old-fashioned methods of achieving these effects – broadcasting a sound into an echo chamber or using a spring – were uncontrollable. They also reduced fidelity.

Electronics engineers knew that an electronic circuit ought to be able to delay a signal – the problem was how? Analog echo devices were built. These successfully delayed the signal for a few milliseconds but provided a rather sharp reverb rather than true echo. Finally, it was digital conversion that provided the answer. The incoming signal was translated into digital information, which could more easily be delayed. There were, and are, problems in ensuring that the fidelity of the signal is of high enough quality, however, modern digital devices offer long delays quite satisfactorily.

But by 1974, as often happens, technology had started to get ahead of itself and presented studio engineers with an apparently impossible problem. This problem manifested itself in the shape of 24-track tape recorders. Since the big step up from 8 to 16-track, which was made around 1970, engineers, producers and musicians had been clamouring for even greater control, keen to break a band's performance down to its smallest individual parts, and the 24 track, considered the optimum solution, crashed into most major studios at the time when glamorous 'pomp' rock was at its height.

This was the period when supergroups were creating concept albums, stringing together instrumentals and large orchestral backings. They expected to overdub ad infinitum as any of the *Yes* albums from the period will bear testimony. Often the engineers were forced to harness two 24-track machines together to offer 46-track capability – two tracks are required for synchronizing the machines – and the musicians piled on the overdubs with reckless abandon. The problem came when the mix was started.

During the late 1960s, and early 1970s, thousands of very badly mixed records flooded into the shops because of the impossible task of handling 16 or more tracks at the mixing stage. I recall spending hour upon hour mixing tracks that were, in reality, completely uncontrollable. In the end, engineers had to develop a system of removing the advantages that big multi-track machines offered in order to handle the mixes. Usually the answer was to do intermediate mixes which removed some of the tracks before the final mix. This completely defeated the object of buying an expensive 24-track machine.

The alternative was that horrific scene in which the engineer, the lead vocalist and the roadie all bent over the desk racked with tension as they each tried to get their little part right for the final mix. Mix after mix failed, tension mounted along with the studio bill and finally the session would disintegrate and everybody would go home. Alternatively, the producer would pronounce himself satisfied with a second-rate mix just to get the bloody job over.

The day was saved by the microprocessor. With hindsight, the task seems ideally suited for computer control, but in 1975, it was as if the sun had risen to reveal the tablets of stone. Within two years every major studio in the world had computer-assisted mixdown and the heady race for better recording technology began again.

One of the earliest computer-controlled desks in Britain was installed at London's Advision Recording Studios. The studio's clients had long been battling with over-complex mixes and the Quad-8 desk that arrived from California was so successful that Advision studio-time became impossible to get.

In the beginning, a computer controlled the fader levels of recording consoles. On the 24-track tape, two tracks had to be left spare to store the computer data. At the start of a mix the engineer would switch the system to 'write' and start a mix. Of course he would be unable to control the 22 faders properly but at the end of the mix the computer had memorized precisely where he had placed the faders at each point during the mix. He could then play back his mix and listen to it. By switching individual tracks to write during playback, he could adjust the level of each track against the rest, adding the new information to the data. In this way he could refine the mix over and again before committing it to master tape. It was the breakthrough everybody had been looking for and multi-track mixes ceased to be a problem – almost over night.

Of course sophistication rapidly piled upon sophistication and today the studio engineer sits at a totally automated desk which will not only recall and physically reproduce all of the fader movements during a mix, but will also recall all equalization alterations and patches. This means that very elaborate mixes are possible. Engineers are free continuously to alter e.q. on tracks throughout the performance of a song and the contribution the microprocessor has made to mixing is equivalent to the impact that multi-track recording made on sound recording in the late 1950s.

Within the next couple of years small computer-assisted consoles will become available for small and home studios. Roland have already produced a multi-purpose automated mixer – The CPE-800 Compu-Editor – and this is the forerunner of inexpensive automated mixers. The large automated desks used in professional recording studios cost around £100,000, and whilst the £1,000 automated desk is still a thing of the future, even today it only takes a few thousand pounds to provide computer power for the smaller studio.

The Roland CPE-800. This 'Compu-Editor' is a flexible automated mixer which can be used to control sound or lights. Coupled with an 8-track tape recorder and a conventional mixer it can provide relatively inexpensive automated mixing in small recording studios.

The CPE-800 offers 15 faders (assignable), built in SMPTE time-code generation — for multi-track synchronization — and several other useful features. A typical studio configuration might be: Teac 8-track, Studiomaster 16 into 4/8 and the CPE-800. Such a package would be considered inexpensive in studio terms.

The Roland unit is not a digital mixer, but is a digital-control unit for an analog mixer. Its internal 32K of RAM and associated microprocessor governs 15 separate voltage control channels which will read information from analog mixer faders and, in turn, supply control information for playback. It is a highly useful tool.

Of course the automation of professional desks allowed their manufacturers to thumb their collective noses at those makers producing microphones and off-line equipment and threw the technological challenge back at the tape recorder manufacturers.

As tape formats grew, so systems of reducing the increasing tape hiss were found. The noise-reduction system invented by Ray Dolby in the 1960s became so important that his name was to be found on almost every tape recorder in the world twenty years later. But the problem of tape noise was not the only problem represented by that medium. Its dynamic range was limited and although better and better tapes were developed which could record sounds ever louder, softer, higher and lower, it was clear that the microprocessor would provide the final answer for recording.

Digital recording has been commercially carried out since 1979. A Bert Kaempfert album was one of the first records to be recorded digitally, and subsequently a large number of artists have issued recordings that at some point in the recording chain were captured digitally.

The advantages of using a digital recorder instead of a tape recorder are significant. The sounds produced by the artists are converted from microphone-type electrical signals into numbers and stored by the computer to be reconverted to electrical signals and replayed. This digital information represents the *precise* sound produced by the trumpets, singers, drums, whatever. There is no colouration from any physical storage medium such as tape and there is virtually no limit to the dynamic range which can be captured. If you have had a chance to hear a digital recording you will have noticed the difference.

Most importantly, digital storage offers the engineer absolute control over the information stored. Very precise editing is possible and there is no risk of making a mistake or of making a noisy edit. Overall controls of such elements as pitch and tempo are easily provided without the speed or pitch problems that existed with analog tape.

One of the major problems facing the makers of digital recording equipment is to make the recorders user friendly. One American manufacturer has gone so far as to offer tape-style editing on a digital machine in a effort to persuade engineers that it is easy to edit on the system. The problem is an ignorance barrier; many people are frightened of computers and so create myths around them that in turn form barriers. Usually a short demonstration softens any prejudice of this sort but, surprisingly, anti-computer reaction is still being encountered in the high-tec world of recording.

You may be surprised to see digital recorders described as digital tape recorders, it would seem a contradiction in terms. The tape used on a digital tape recorder is not storing analog electrical information, it is storing digital data in much the same way as an IBM mainframe computer uses large reels of tape.

Another of the problems besetting the manufacturers of digital tape recorders is the lack of an accepted international standard for the sampling rate.

'Sampling rate' is the term which describes how often, in a given period of time (a second, for example), the computer 'looks' at the wave form it is to reproduce as numbers. The shape of the wave form is measured at given intervals, perhaps every one hundredth of a second, and each measurement is given a numeric value. Thus, digitally stored sound is a large collection of numbers which represents the highs and lows of a sound wave. Obviously, it is reasonable to ask what is going on during the split seconds between measurement and it is this basic problem that leads to the discussion of sampling rate.

The more often a computer measures the shape of the sound wave, the more complete its numerical picture becomes. Luckily, sound waves have very few anomalies in the range that is audible to the human ear. In general a sound wave slopes up and then down and even variations such as square waves, still follow this basic pattern. In very high frequencies (well outside of human hearing) abrupt peaks occur, but for audio purposes these can be ignored.

So, designers of audio digital equipment can safely rely on the fact that with a sampling rate of 100,000 times a second, no important part of the sound wave is going to be missed. But measuring the wave shape this often and storing the resultant numbers takes up a lot of memory. It also means that a five minute single tone could require 30,000 separate numbers. If that sound were complex — music for example — and full of separate sound waves the 30,000 could quite easily rise to 300,000 and above. Despite the power of current computers, this would tax many machines to the limit and would leave little instant memory capacity for other functions such as control over sound and routing systems.

Thankfully, there is a way round it. A low pass filter effectively allows use of rates as low as 40-50,000 times a second. This filter gets rid of waves outside of the required spectrum (those above human hearing, etc) and makes possible an accurate transference from sound to numbers — analog to digital — at a much lower sampling rate.

Measurement of a sound and its conversion into digital information suitable for computer storage is done in a separate unit from the computer itself. This piece of equipment is called an ADC (analog to digital converter) and when the digitally stored information requires re-conversion to analog form, perhaps to drive a loudspeaker, it has to be processed through a DAC (digital to analog converter.)

The problem that exists in the world of recording is that manufacturers and expert bodies cannot agree on what should be the standard sampling rate — or indeed on how to store the digital information. Using a good low pass filter high quality sound can be obtained at around 20K samples per second (20KHz). However, professional studios need a much higher sampling rate to eliminate as much distortion as possible, but, of course, high sampling rates eat memory. The sampling rates in current use are 48K, which is regarded by many engineers as the 'professional rate' for recording, and 44.1K which has been adopted by Sony-Philips, clear leaders amongst manufacturers in the digital recording field. To confound the situation still further, the European Broadcasting Union have settled on a sampling rate of 32K for digital audio broadcast transmission.

The problem is that equipment using different sampling rates does not interface easily. Imagine a superstar's album recorded digitally at 48K arriving in the cutting room where all the digital record-cutting equipment works at 44.1K.

Although equipment is now on the market to interface 48K and 44.1K systems, it is rather a silly situation and hopefully it will have been resolved by the time you read this.

Some audio specialists feel that even the 48K sampling rate is too low, but it is likely to be the standard that studios will settle for and the industry as a whole will continue with dual standards for some time. But it is not always right to judge a digital recording system by sampling rate alone. While there is a basic truth in the argument that the more often a computer looks at and measures a soundwave the more accurate the digital representation of that sound will be, consideration must be given to the ability of the filters and other peripheral components. In his masterwork *Musical Applications of Microprocessors*, Hal Chamberlin remarks that a single sine wave can be represented accurately in digital form at only 2K if a very good low pass filter is available. As an aside, the introduction of full digital recording will hasten the end of the record as we know it. The final limitations of vinyl as an information medium are fast being reached and the public are already being offered music on a form of digital disk. Other systems will be developed and in the new hi-fi chain, conversion into analog won't occur until the sound is being sent out to the loudspeakers. The difference in sound will be startling as will the flexibility of handling – remember David Bowie's 'music spheres' in *The Man Who Fell To Earth*?

The second standards problem besetting the recording industry is the means of storing the digital information on tape. At the moment, a conventionally recorded 24-track tape can be taken off a machine in San Francisco, carried on board a plane and flown to Munich, for example, where it could be put straight on to another 24-track machine and be replayed almost instantly.

Tapes on a digital recorder, however, store the numbers the computer uses to interpret sound. Each manufacturer has his own method of storing digital information on tape and the tape made in San Francisco would be useless in Munich unless the machines were of the same make.

But, as you probably know, the micro is now being linked to telecommunications. In theory, the equipment exists for the studio in San Francisco to phone the studio in Munich, connect the digital recorder to the telephone and transmit the information – the songs. The studio in Munich receives the call, plugs it into their digital recorder and the information is duplicated in Munich and can be replayed, no matter which two digital recorders are used. The music that is contained in the digital recorder in Munich will sound identical to the San Francisco music, there will be *no* deterioration during transfer as the numbers at each end will be identical. The big drawback to this idyllic state of affairs is that information transmission via a telephone line is currently very slow. Improvements in telecommunications, particularly the introduction of fibre-optic carriers, will reduce the time taken and a transfer of an album will be possible in an hour or so.

It will certainly be cheaper and safer than flying the digital master tape from SF to Munich, and it becomes obvious that the whole concept of one master tape, and copies from it, will disappear. If the original digital recording can be replicated endlessly without the smallest loss of quality there will quickly be confusion over which collection of numbers is the master. By the end of the 1980s major recording studios and record companies will be able to pass their entire catalog of music around the world via the phone service, *if* they choose to!

The use of easy communications for a property such as music raises the problem of copyright theft, which is a subject touched on elsewhere in this book with regard to computer programs. If a record company is sending, say, a new album by Stevie Wonder down the phone lines to the record-cutting plant, it would be easy for it to be intercepted and copied. As explained, the copy won't be an inferior bootleg but a perfect replica of the real thing.

It is also a relatively easy matter for the digital recording to be copied at any point in the chain of creation, from recording studio, record company, artist, music publisher, management company – in fact anywhere that the information exists in digital form.

This will be a major problem and one that will not be easy to solve. One of the main problems that is likely to prohibit the introduction of digital recording for the home user is the ease with which digital recordings can be copied. Records can now be copied on to cassette tapes and this has been worrying record companies for some years, but digital storage allows perfect reproductions to be made instantly. The very concept of digital makes this possible. If the digital information has to be off-loaded from a storage device into a record-playing system then logically the digital information can be loaded on to another suitable medium, another chip, a disk drive, a cassette, etc. Naturally, manufacturers are developing ways of defeating this, principally by developing hardware storage devices that are incompatible with standard mass-storage systems.

It is also true to say that all digital music instruments are theoretically capable of exchanging information by phone (when transfer speed is sufficient). It is realistic to consider a future recording session that could develop in the following way: the trumpet player is sent the track down the phone to his home from the studio. He decodes it on his digital recorder and listens to it. He plays his part, records it digitally and sends it back down the phone lines to the studio.

It is highly unlikely that much music will be made in this way (for other than experimental reasons), as most musicians prefer to work together. Alternatively, with the arrival of systems like the Fairlight (see Chapter 9), there would seem to be no need for a trumpet player to play any part at all.

There are, however, still some problems with digital recording. In conventional tape recording background noise is the major problem against which engineers have to fight. This background noise has not been completely eliminated in digital recording. Whilst it is obvious that the computer itself does not introduce noise, there is a new noise to contend with in recording. The numeric value the computer gives to each measurement of the sound wave is finite, only a set number of digits is available to represent the measurement, thus the measurement has a roundoff error. The industry call this quantization error because the measurement has been quantized to the nearest number. This error appears as noise in the audio spectrum.

Technology has now reduced this error to the point where the quality of digitally produced sound already far exceeds that available by any other means. Undoubtedly this error will shrink into insignificance in all but the highest-level (e.g. laboratory) applications within the very near future.

Despite the various limitations outlined above, digital recording has started to catch on in a big way. Most of the major international studios convert analog to digital at some link in the chain – not just in digital delays – and the race is on to develop the all-digital studio. At the moment, the recording industry is going through a period of transition with many producers and engineers resisting the lure of digital sound perfection until the technology is complete.

Martin Rushent, producer of the Human League is typical: 'I want to wait until it is all digital – until it gets converted into digital in the microphone capsule and doesn't come back into analog until the record is cut. I can't see any point in converting backwards and forwards, because the moment you go into analog you're defeating all the marvellous things you get out of digital!'

Not all producers agree. Paul McCartney's album *Tug Of War* was recorded multi-track analog in Air Studios, London and in the Bahamas. Geoff Emerick then mixed the LP on to the PCM-1610 digital audio processor in London. The record was cut in New York using the Sony DDU-1520 digital preview unit, the CBS DISComputer and the Sony PCM digital audio processor. In simple language, Emerick used computer control to beat some of the limitations of vinyl records and enhance the dynamics of the cut (get more volume on to it). The result of this application of digital technology was a cut 3dB louder.

Going digital during recording also allows the recording team superior editing control, and this benefit is considerable in applications such as film music and TV commercials where editing is a major part of music production.

The DSP, a fully-digital recording studio console by Neve Electronics, which is claimed to be the first of its kind in the world. All sound is controlled digitally and this allows engineers to move sound within the 'time domain' of a track. This desk was installed at the BBC Television Centre in London in 1982.

In the race for the all-digital studio, the British company, Neve, have produced one of the first all-digital desks. Most desks in semi-digital studios only accept analog input, requiring conventional electronic signals for processing. Neve has developed an all-digital mixing desk, the DSP Console.

For engineers brought up to expect the flight-deck appearance of modern analog consoles, the DSP and other digital mixing desks will come as something of a shock – there appear to be very few controls. The reason is that all controls are assignable – they each have several functions and are under the control of a microprocessor.

The sound captured by the microphones is converted to digital form and enters the DSP desk in this way. Whilst in the desk, the sound remains stored in digital form and as it is independent of the live event – information being stored as it is received – the information enters non-real-time. This means that events, a trumpet solo for example, can be moved *within the time domain* of the track for significant effects.

In completing the digital chain, the console ensures the highest audio quality – Neve claim that the DSP's audio specifications approach the maximum theoretical limit – with enormous editing flexibility. Microprocessors are also able to help with studio design and construction. The acoustic measurement of recording environments is important and spectrum analyzers have been the usual tool applied to the task of indicating the harmonic response curve of a studio. The microprocessor is now able to assist the designer or engineer by building a graphic, 3D, display from the results of spectrum analysis, offering a clear representation on the acoustics of the recording environment. Typical of these systems is the Eventide Real Time Audio Spectrum analyzer which is a software package available with interfaces for Apple, TRS-80 and Commodore microcomputers. This system displays a multi-dimensional graph of acoustic responses and when work is being carried out on the environment, reference to the computer screen allows judgements to be made about the effectiveness of acoustic treatments. For the musician who already owns a compatible microcomputer, such a system would prove a valuable tool for analyzing the response of musical instruments and recording or performing environments.

The micro has also assisted the recording process in an indirect way. The control over music-making that is described in the other chapters in this book allows musicians and producers to save considerable amounts of recording studio time. In a complex song, many parts can be pre-programmed into the relevant instrument for reproduction in the studio. Once a basic rhythm has been established – on a Linn Drum or similar (see Chapter 4) – melody lines, chords, bass, etc may all be programmed into sequencers well in advance of the session. During recording the pre-programmed parts will be replayed and, thus, the maximum amount of studio time can be diverted to any live performance that has to be captured, e.g. vocals or special live instrumentals.

This method is having an effect on the design of new recording studios. Traditionally, studios have been designed with large studio areas and smaller control rooms. The latest studios are being built with large control rooms and small studios. All of the programmed music is fed into the recorder by direct input and only individual elements, such as overdubbed acoustic drums or vocals, are added in the studio. The days of the group sitting around in an adapted stage-type situation has gone.

The micro has also changed production techniques. Martin Rushent works with the Human League in a way that would have been impossible a few years ago.

After hearing the song to be recorded, Rushent works out a bar chart, logging the chord changes, tempo changes and so on. With the League he then puts a timecode on to a multi-track tape machine using a Roland MC-8 MicroComposer. Next he enters a basic rhythm track into a Linn Drum, adds that to the multi-track and then programs a bass part into a synthesizer which is also added to the tape. The main melodies on the track are then programmed and recorded and the vocals are laid down. Last of all, the drums will be recorded. These may be drum sounds from the Linn Drum or acoustic drums. The traditional procedures for recording have been reversed. Every single note put on a Human League record is considered, there's no chance that a musician will play a good solo one day and a bad one the next. Inspiration for melody composition during programming may be better one day than the next, but as I emphasized in Chapter 1, this is an example of the shift in emphasis away from the performer to the composer.

All of the above is altering the nature of recording as it has been practised for twenty years. The studio is becoming a processing plant with much of the music made at other locations.

The trend in music is similar to the trends in every other area affected by computers, it is a trend towards isolationism. It is possible to build a picture of a musician who is capable of playing every instrument with computer aid, and who can then record it perfectly in his or her own home. Transmission of the recording, whether to an aunt or a record company, will be achieved through the phone line or cable.

It is worth repeating that this mental picture does not require the musician to be rich, the price of microprocessors is falling so rapidly that micro-power should be available to the vast majority within a few years.

4 The Micro as Teacher

Press any note on the keyboard: the note sounds and pops on to a musical staff on the screen, its notational name appearing over it. If you hold the note for one beat, the note sounds for one beat and appears as a quarter note (crotchet), if you hold it longer, it will become a half note (minim). Press another note, then another and another and the music witten on the staff moves over to let the new notes in. When you've finished, press 'play' and the computer will play it back to you at any tempo you desire. If you've made a mistake, delete the note that is wrong and then listen to the piece again. Continue this process until the piece is perfect.

Try something else: order the piece to be played back in tuition mode. Now the first note appears on the screen and you have to find the same note on your keyboard. The note won't sound until you have found the right note and pressed it. Then the next note appears and you have to find the right note again and so on.

Computers are revolutionizing the teaching of music. With a system such as this, who wouldn't be able to learn musical theory in a few days?

Micro aids for music teaching/learning are now available priced from under a hundred dollars (well under £50) to a few thousand. But even the inexpensive models do suprising things.

Music students may be classified in three groups: a) children, b) young people (aged 14-24) and c) adults who wish to play for leisure. Not surprisingly, manufacturers produce instruments dedicated to the needs of each individual group. But the micro is so powerful that children's instruments can fascinate professional musicians, and home organs − for long considered anathema by professional musicians − are now capable of emitting high quality, digitally-produced tones that are far better than many latterday professional performance instruments.

Computer-based instruments intended to assist learning fall into two sub-categories: dedicated and non-dedicated. The dedicated instruments are usually portable and inexpensive. The non-dedicated instruments are software systems designed to be used with home computers. Although the non-dedicated systems aren't as portable as the smaller dedicated instruments, they are more powerful and often take the student further along the path to musical proficiency.

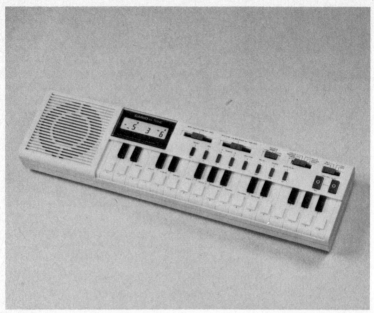

The Casio VL-Tone. This little pocket instrument surprised the musical world in 1981 when it was produced. It was inexpensive, yet it was able to remember tunes entered, and play back compositions at varying tempos. The development of a 'dedicated' VLSI allowed the company to market the instrument so cheaply.

The musical world was shocked in the summer of 1981 when Casio, a Japanese company previously best known for calculators and watches, launched a tiny, $70 (£35) computer instrument called the VL-Tone.

Only just over 11 x 5 in. (28 x 12.5cm), the battery-powered VL-Tone can record up to 100 notes and then play them back at the pitch, rhythm and tempo of the student's choice with an appropriate, automatically provided, rhythm accompaniment. There are a choice of 10 types of rhythm and the balance between the rhythm and the melody may be adjusted. Five voices allow the user to select sounds from piano, synthesizer, violin, flute or guitar or ADSR sounds. ADSR (an acronym for the stages of the amplitude of a sound: attack, decay, sustain, release) is a surprising feature on such an inexpensive instrument and selection of this sound base allows users to create their own sound, whilst learning about the nature of sound itself.

In all fairness, it must be pointed out that this tiny plastic instrument can't produce high-quality sounds from its minute internal speaker, but they are quite acceptable when heard over headphones or with a reasonable hi-fi system. In addition to offering considerable musical power, the instrument becomes a full-feature calculator at the touch of a switch with auto-shut down for battery preservation.

Casio achieved all of this by making a massive investment to produce a VLSI (very large scale integrated circuit) dedicated to music making. Casio said at the time that they had to sell one million VL-Tones to recover the investment, but that target is now reported as having been reached. The development of such a chip has had a significant effect on other musical instruments now in the company's range, and has led to the introduction of some extremely clever instruments.

VLSIs such as the one developed by Casio are complete computers. Micro-lithography advances have enabled engineers to build all of the elements of the computer – central processing unit, arithmetical control, etc – inside the same tiny device. Only subsidiary circuits such as memory store, input and output facilities and power supply are external.

The VL-Tone delighted many forward-thinking educationalists by its interactive encouragement. Children can take an unknown piece of written music, enter it as slowly as they choose into the VL-Tone's memory and then hear it played back at the correct tempo. This leads to an understanding of the relationship between actual music and its written language which would otherwise only develop over a long period of time.

An important feature of the VL-Tone is 'One Key Play.' After entering a sequence of the notes, the student may tap this key to hear each note in sequence. The faster the student taps, the faster he or she hears the notes. The longer the student holds the button down, the longer the note sounds. From this it will be seen that by tapping the key and holding it down for appropriate periods of time, a real appreciation of the musical function of time and note length may be built up.

The musical input keys on the VL-Tone can't be considered as offering any chance to acquire keyboard skills – they are, in reality, buttons laid out in keyboard configuration. Despite the limitation of the 29 keys provided, a total sound range of two and a half octaves is available by use of a transposition switch.

The Casiotone CT-401 is typical of the 'home keyboard' that is replacing the electronic easy-play spinet organ as a popular purchase. These small keyboards have the ability to remember tunes and allow editing to take place after the player or composer has performed the piece.

In a rather crass sales pitch, to a mass market of adults who Casio perceive as being musically frustrated, the company describes the VL-Tone as its 'technological gift to the ungifted.' Perhaps they are right – but its role in stimulating gifted young minds may end up being its most important contribution.

Other manufacturers were not slow to follow Casio's lead and today there are a variety of inexpensive, instrument/toys on the market. Each has particular selling points and some pay more attention to educational aspects than others.

Yamaha's HandySound HS-500 is a small, plastic instrument which encourages learning by operating a points scoring system on most of its five games. The HandySound has the advantage of having a real keyboard spanning a 25 note range. It is also capable of sounding four notes together enabling chords to be played.

'Match It' is a game in which note names appear in the liquid crystal display and the student musician is expected to find the relevant key. There are several levels of skill that may be selected, beginner, intermediate and advanced and at the end of a sequence the display will show how many notes were right out of a possible total. At the more advanced level the student is given very little time in which to find the right notes.

Another game, 'Pairs,' plays two notes and then expects the student to play them. Once again, there are three levels of skill and a score provided. 'Chord Chase' is a useful ear-training feature. In this game, the HandySound plays a chord which the student then has to play. At the beginning the instrument provides 'hints' about which notes are contained in the chords but these disappear as the game progresses. If the player makes a mistake twice on the notes of the chord the right combination of notes is displayed. Top score in this game is 100 points. A second game useful for ear training is called 'Copy Cat.' In this game the instrument plays a seven or eight note melody and the student has to repeat it exactly. Points are also awarded for this game.

The final game in the Handysound HS-500 is for two players and is called 'Musical Tennis.' In this game a note is bounced up the keyboard and the second player has to bounce it back by playing the right note. Scoring in this game is as per tennis with deuce and advantage points!

Tools like this are immensely powerful for teaching the 6-13 age group – larger models offer eight note polyphony and sounds equitable with major synthesizers. Within a very short time, the successful development of inexpensive speech simulators and input devices will produce instruments that 'sing' the right note names and which produce a tune from a sung input. Larger keyboards already contain tell tale lights guiding the fingers into the right positions on the keyboard and Casio have produced a range of keyboards that can read music from specially-produced bar charts. A light-pen is fitted to these instruments which reads a bar code – similar to product identification bar codes – and loads this digital information. When required, the instrument will reproduce the information as music.

Within a few years we can expect to see a small keyboard that has sufficient memory capacity to house a software program which can take a beginner from zero to accomplished player with all the steps built in. Keyboards will instruct on technique, timing and expression and human teachers will be freed to study music development paths, choice of material and individual expression.

One aspect in this dramatic change in musical tuition that worries traditionalists is that some of the conventional instruments are likely to lose popularity with children. A keyboard, alphanumeric or musical, is an excellent input device for a computer and the majority of computer-based musical instruments will be based on keyboards. Traditional instruments such as the violin, which require many months of practice before pleasing sounds may be produced, may stand little chance of holding a child's attention against the significant attraction of playing musical games with a keyboard-controlled computer toy.

It is, perhaps, arguable that an understanding of musical theory should be arrived at before a young student starts developing technique on a particular instrument, but with the ability of the microchip to store the sound of a violin and reproduce it perfectly, what incentive is there that will produce the recruits for the Suzuki violin method?

Obviously, some parents will go on steering their children towards conventional instruments, but unless society reacts against the mechanization of music-making (not of music itself) it seems likely that far fewer children will become accomplished on traditional instruments in the medium to long-term future. This leads to the conclusion that classical music and other music written for traditional instruments will either be performed by fewer musicians – and therefore by fewer good players – or, more likely, that the musician's role will be partly taken over by the programmed music computer (see Chapter 9). The only area likely to remain inviolate is live performance: in all recording situations – broadcasts, recording sessions etc – arrangers and composers will program computers to create the music.

Using your home computer to run a music program is an excellent method of learning about musical theory and although the cheaper programs have little facility for teaching keyboard technique, their ability to teach musical theory is excellent. Interaction is the principal advantage these non-dedicated systems offer and the power available is entirely dependent upon the memory capacity of your computer and the thoroughness of the program.

Home computers can be purchased from as little as $100 up to $5,000 (about £50 — £2,500.) The smallest computers are capable of running music programs and with some technical knowledge on the part of the user, many are capable of controlling a synthesizer.

One of the friendliest musical programs for small computers is 'The Musician' which is manufactured by the Philips company for their G7000 Videopac Computer. The computer sells in Britain for well under £100, the program for £30 and the system plugs into the aerial

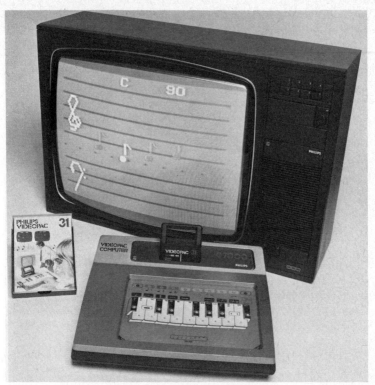

One of the least expensive computer-music packages is the G7000 'Videopac'
computer from Philips with the 'Musician' software cartridge. Although too
limited for any serious musical use, the program is perfect for teaching the
rudiments of music and helps children understand the relationship between time
and melody.

socket of a regular domestic television set.

The price of this home computer has been kept down by utilizing a
touch-sensitive printed alphanumeric keyboard similar to Sinclair's
and this is the only drawback to an otherwise excellent system.

The Musician program arrives with a card printed to represent a 16
note piano keyboard. This card fits over the typewriter-style
keyboard on the computer for the duration of the program's use,
effectively dedicating the computer to musical use. The touch-

sensitive keyboard works perfectly for normal computer work, but when converted for musical use, the player must develop positive fingering to avoid mistakes. Designers of touch-sensitive keyboards have to ensure that the keys are not over-sensitive and this requires that the user is accurate in his or her key strokes. To be fair, Philips make no suggestion that The Musician is a serious musical instrument. It is a teaching tool and as such is excellent.

Philips have opted to develop their own kind of software pack, rather than offer the typical cassette interface found in most small home computers. Philips software comes supplied in a plug-in cartridge which is pushed into a slot at the front of the computer. Although this restricts the computer's flexibility (you can only use Philips software packs in the system) it provides a child-proof method of handling computer information and this is an important element in a teaching tool.

On inserting the Musician pack, placing the keyboard card over the alphanumeric keyboard and switching on, the TV screen becomes green and two musical staves appear with treble and bass clefs. The keyboard has an octave transpose function which allows the musician the use of 32 notes, although the printed card represents only 16.

Two modes of music playing are possible: 'real-time' and 'recorded.' If the player starts to press notes whilst the screen is green, he is playing the keyboard as he would any normal keyboard instrument. As each note is pressed, the corresponding note appears on the screen.

The tones produced by the computer are clean and clear without any of the unpleasant hard edges sometimes produced by computers. There are no frills to the sound production system. It is impossible to add vibrato, or to alter the sustain of a note. When a C is pressed, a C sounds for as long as it is held. The two dimensional 'card keyboard' accurately displays full-size piano-type notes, but normal keyboard technique is out of the question. The best method is to play it with an index finger. Each note has its name printed on the key with sharps and flats designated as C, E- and so on.

Pressing a control on the keyboard changes the screen to red and the player enters the record mode. In this mode a time value appears in the top right hand corner of the screen and a metronome is heard. The time expression is in quarter notes (crotchets) per minute and this may be infinitely varied so that the metronome speeds up or slows down as the player requires.

After setting the right rhythm, the player begins to play as if he were playing a normal instrument. In practice, the best method of playing is to use written music and to enter the notes from the music – quite a few pieces are provided in the instruction book. 'Speed Music' or other easy-play music written with the note names contained in the notes themselves make this an easy process for the student. Using the metronome as a reference, the individual notes may be held for the correct number of beats and the corresponding note value will appear on the staff. Thus a student who presses A and holds it down for two and a half beats will see a dotted half note (minimum) appear at the A position on the staff. Whether it appears on the treble or bass staff depends on which octave has been selected by the transpose control (treble is the default choice). When the student plays the next note it appears in the corresponding position on the staff and the notes begin to 'scroll' off to the left of the screen as the music progresses. Four or five notes may be seen on the screen at one time. When no note is played, a rest appears, equivalent to the amount of time passed without a note being played. Real-time playing is converted by the computer into notes, note lengths, rhythms and rests. There are no mathematical values attached to any part of the program. The student hears and sees what he or she plays.

Of course, a student will make many mistakes while trying to play the music. In the record mode the computer will store up to 81 notes and when the memory is full the screen will automatically turn green again. When the student has finished the first attempt at playing a tune, or when the computer memory has been used up, the student may hear how well the piece went. Pressing another button changes the screen to blue and the music replays precisely as it was entered. The notes appear on the staff and scroll leftwards as the music progresses, with the note actually being sounded taking on a greater luminosity on the screen. Beginners will have fluffed some notes and will have mistimed others. They may listen to their attempts as often as they choose and may compare the results of their playing as shown on the screen with the written music in front of them. Students may then correct their mistakes.

The computer's editing power in music is one of its greatest uses. The player may 'step' through the piece that has been entered by pressing a button to hear each note individually. When he or she reaches the first note that is wrong, or has an incorrect time value (the note-type is shown on the screen), the player may delete it by one button push and open the insert mode. Pressing the insert button changes the screen to red and switches the recording mode and the metronome back on. Using this beat, the player can adjust to the rhythm and then press the correct note holding it for the required number of beats. The program always rounds the pressed time up or down to the nearest musical time value, automatically compensating for the player's inaccuracies.

When the student has played the new note correctly — if it is still wrong the procedure can be repeated — the piece may be heard from the start again and the student may step through it until the second wrong note is reached. In this way the student may create a perfect piece of music from a ragged first attempt and, in the process, learn about time, note values and note positions.

As a student becomes more skilled, he or she may edit music out of real-time. Instead of playing the note to be inserted in a real-time mode, he may use a time value button and then enter the time value the notes should have had via the numeric keys provided at the top of the overlay card. Four beats (a semi-breve or semi-breve rest) are signified by the number 8. Three beats by 6, two by 4, one and a half by 3 and so on down to half beats (quavers) by 1. Using this form of input the student can correct a piece of music without having to play it through endlessly.

The piece may be recorded at a slow metronome setting, edited to perfection and then be replayed at any speed the student desires — without any pitch change. There is no facility for storing the music in the program and the results of each session are lost when the computer is switched off.

Several other tuition aids are programmed into this clever software. The student may replay the piece that has been entered in a mode which forces him to identify the names of the notes correctly. The first few notes of the melody appear on the screen and the first note is 'lit up.' A question mark appears in the space that usually identifies the note and the student has to press the correct note on the keyboard in order for the note to sound and the next note to light up. There are three pre-programmed tunes in the software cartridge which may be replayed in the same way. A note appears on the staff and the student has to press the corresponding note on the keyboard before the note will sound. When the student has successfully identified the string of notes the piece will play through until stopped.

A further music-reading aid is built-in using the computer's random capability. In this mode the computer places notes on the staff at random and the student has to press the corresponding note on the keyboard before the note sounds and the next note appears. This is excellent training as the notes move in and out of the bass and treble clef completely at random, testing the student's sight reading to the full. When some basic ability at reading has been mastered, yet another sight-reading aid is available to further develop the skill. The random capability may be used to generate a string of notes which cascade out without their identification names being shown above. The tempo of this string may be controlled by the built-in metronome and the student may identify the notes at any tempo he chooses.

A full range of built-in scales is provided in the program. Pressing the transpose control, followed by the root note of the scale desired, sets the computer up to deliver the scale when the 'scale button' is pushed. Scales starting from any note on the keyboard are executed perfectly with the corresponding notation appearing on the screen. For musicians in non-English speaking territories, the program has variations embedded into the program which take into account national differences — the tonic sol-fa system and its linguistic equivalents. Users select their own language system at the start of the program. The Musician is typical of small computer programs now appearing on the market. It is cheap, flexible and provides a thorough grounding in musical theory. Above all, it is fun.

The larger home computer has enormous power to control music. The subject is dealt with more extensively in Chapter 7 where serious music-making programs and systems for home computers are discussed, but it is worthwhile commenting here on the programs which are written for musical tuition and fun and which will run on home computers.

With the exception of the 'popular' end of the market containing such computers as the Sinclair ZX81 and the Philips G7000 Videopac, most home computers have a power range of between 8K and 64K. The smaller computers sell for a few hundred dollars whilst the 64K models can easily start at $5,000 before any peripherals such as printers are purchased. Popular brands in this category are Radio Shack TRS-80, Apple, Commodore Pet, Sharp, etc. At the time of writing the more expensive models in this category are about to become obsolete — although still very useful — as the new '16-bit' units arrive on the market.

The IBM Personal computer was the first large-capacity home computer to utilize the new generation 16-bit chips. These microprocessors are faster and more powerful than the current 8-bit chips and the new generation of home computers will typically offer 128K of RAM for similar money. This kind of computing power will allow very sophisticated music-tuition programs to be developed, but because of the 'software gap' (the fact that our hardware achievements are outstripping our own ability to harness the power) it may be sometime before really clever programs are available to get the best from the power.

Within a few years, however, it is likely that software programs will exist to turn an inexpensive home computer into a fully digital synthesizer of the type described in Chapter 9. In addition, these systems will be able to take dictation from a sung melody and convert it into instant music and will be interactive in tuition situations to an incredible degree.

One of the present day's most popular computers is the Apple. Now in the 'Apple 11 plus' version, it is the computer that most music-

The Apple II with the 'Musicomp' composition display on the monitor. The 'Musicomp' is the least expensive non-real-time composition program available for the Apple, producing tones entirely from software control.

oriented companies have chosen to use as a base for computer music systems. Several of the systems are designed for professional use and these are described in Chapter 7, but several are also intended as tuition aids. The advanced – and excellent – alphaSyntauri music teaching system is discussed later, but 'Musicomp,' a simpler music program for Apples allows the owner of a 32k Apple computer to use the system to compose music for a program cost of around $60. The program is best described as an intermediate tutor for students interested in composition.

The main problem in running a music program with a home computer is that there are no basic parts of the computer circuit capable of generating musical tones. In the professional music systems new boards are added to the computer and these contain circuits capable of producing analog or digital synthesizer type sounds, but in simple home computers tone generation is either non-existent or very limited. When home computers have greater RAM capacity this will cease to be a problem, as external sounds from the natural world will be analyzed and stored digitally by the computer, using analog to digital converters. (See Chapter 9 for a description of how this type of sound production is being carried out today by dedicated music computers).

The system necessary to run the Musicomp is an Apple with a minimum RAM of 32K, one disk drive and a language or integer card added inside the computer. Each item is available separately from Apple and easily fitted by the user. Package cost is likely to work out less than £1,500 ($3,000).

The Musicomp program is supplied on a four and a quarter inch floppy disk and running requires no preparation other than booting up the system.

The 'cassette out' mini-jack socket at the back of the Apple may be connected to the input of an audio amplifier, although the program will run with the tiny internal speaker.

The program is menu driven (see Chapter 9 for full explanation of this type of software) and students are prompted to enter their requirements from the Apple's alphanumeric keyboard. The Musicomp program is totally different in concept from lower-level programs such as The Musician, by Philips. The program assumes that the student understands musical theory and knows how to work a computer. Some programming experience is necessary, and without a basic knowledge of how computer systems run, it would be impossible to get this program up and running without assistance. The manual provided with the program is a major hindrance to this program's friendliness. In the future, greater effort will undoubtedly be made towards improving program friendliness but, for the moment, many software packages are based on the assumption that the user is capable of understanding the program author's intention from abysmal and often quirky descriptive prose. Writing manuals to accompany computer programs is a new craft with few skilled practitioners. The refining method most commonly used at the moment is to distribute a program accompanied by the author's first attempt at describing how to use it and wait for questions and complaints to arise.

All queries are noted and a revised manual is prepared. This is distributed as soon as possible and as the increasing number of owners do increasingly stupid things with the program, so the feedback assists the author or the parent company in preparing a definitive manual. The years that lapse between the launch of the program and the arrival at a thoroughly researched manual can be confusing and frustrating for users of the program who are not well-versed in computer programming.

Large corporations – Tandy, Xerox, IBM – spend fortunes researching manuals before the programs are distributed. This is a point worth remembering when paying the higher prices that these companies tend to charge for programs. Another reason for poor manual writing is that program authors find themselves called on to write a description of their work in clear prose – a skill for which they may have little facility. As a result manuals are usually ill written and often quirky to the point of insanity, and riddled with cliches. Novices outnumber computer experts by thousands to one and a good manual is vital to the 'interface' between computers and humans.

Despite the above criticism, Musicomp is a good inexpensive program which no doubt by now has a revised manual. The program produces three 'voices' from the Apple without the aid of a sound generation board. As a result, there is little tonal variation between the three square waves produced, but the voices offer the ability to change the basic sound into a hard, attacking sound or a softer 'woodwind' sound. The large memory capacity of the Apple allows a store of up to 8,000 notes, making extended melody storage possible. The program is monophonic – it can create only one sound at one time – and must be regarded as a melody instrument – chords are not possible. The biggest lack in the program is a time base. The student is forced to use the tempo arbitrarily set by the program. All music is entered and edited from the alphanumeric keyboard, the keys being converted by the program to represent individual notes. There is no musical type keyboard in the system.

The Musicomp program is really a main program and a sub-program. The main program organizes events, the sub-program creates the music and allows editing. On booting up the Musicomp logo appears on the screen, a sharp pointillistic melody is played as a signature and the program is loaded. The screen displays the opening menu. This lists a selection of titles that the author has created for purposes of demonstrations. The user may move the cursor down the list and select tunes he wishes to hear. Most are classical baroque-type melodies pointillistic in nature such as fugues and minuets. The pieces are a couple of minutes long and when entered, a tied treble and bass staff appears on the screen. The notes of the piece enter the staves from the right-hand side of the screen, the note being played always being the new entry on the right. There is no system of highlighting the note actually being played in the program. The demonstration pieces illustrate the three voices available and familiarize the user with the system. The graphics representing the staves and the notes are excellent.

From the opening menu the student may use the cursor to select 'Add New Music' and it is at this point that the main sub-program is loaded. An empty musical staff appears on the screen (treble and bass clefs) and the student may begin making music. A four-octave range of notes is available, D below the bass clef to D above treble.

The first prompt that appears asks the student to set a mode (the voice that will be used for the note) and the student can type in the appropriate letter to denote which voice is required. The second prompt asks how long the note will be. This question refers to the time value of each note, half note, quarter note, etc, and when this is entered the note itself may be entered.

In the Musicomp program the letters of the alphanumeric keyboard become notes. Middle C is W for example. A sharp above middle C is U. The student is referred to a scale in the manual which sets out the position of each note on the keyboard. This scale had not been printed in my manual but working through each key and writing down the notes that appeared allowed me to create my own scale.

Once this has been done it is easy to select the note required. As the key is pressed so the note sounds (in the voice stipulated) and appears on the staff. If the next note has the same time value and is intended to have the same voice, the next key stroke will enter the next note. If, as is likely, the next note does not have the same time value, the mode control must be re-entered, the voicing reaffirmed or altered and the new time value set, after which the note may be entered.

At first, writing music with the Musicomp program is laborious, each note entered requiring several keystrokes with the added uncertainty of which key represents which note. After a while, these details are remembered and the input from the alphanumeric keyboard becomes quite rapid. After considerable use, the student automatically identifies each note with its keyboard letter and can enter the notes at high speed.

Whilst the entry is progressing the student composer can review his work. Care must be taken to ensure that the right keystrokes are used to call 'review' as the wrong order of commands causes the system to 'lockout.' A lockout in a computer is a checkmate situation in which the arithmetic and the logic units in the computer 'lock out' from memory as a result of attempting to get into the memory simultaneously. The only answer to a lockout is to turn the whole system off and start again. The consequence of this is that all of the music entered in the new session is lost as the student will not have caused it to be 'saved to disk.' Despite a warning printed in the Musicomp manual, this is a serious flaw and is typical of early home computer programs. These program faults damage the reputation of domestic computing and put the technology back on the level of an enthusiast's hobby.

Once the piece of music has been entered into the Musicomp program it is wise for a student to save it on the floppy disk. This is easily done through the secondary control menu and the student may then recall the piece for editing.

Editing is clumsy with Musicomp. Each note is displayed as though it were a line in a computer program. The notes may be altered or be assigned new time or voice values by correcting the appropriate line number, as if the student were writing a computer program. The main problem with this method, apart from the altered perspective on the music, is that there is no way the student can see or hear the music as a whole whilst the editing process is under way. Each time a note is edited, the student may exit the editing mode and re-enter the playing mode to hear the results of the edit, but it is an inflexible system.

The sounds produced by the Apple/Musicomp combination are not particularly pleasant and under any serious amplification betray a sound similar to 'key thump' which rather spoils the music.

From the above it might be assumed that the program is pretty poor; this is not the case. For an existing Apple owner, the small investment for Musicomp is a negligible investment and the return, the ability to write music in the abstract and hear it replayed, is significant.

Most other home computer manufacturers either distribute or recommend music programs to use with their computers.

The giant Texas Instruments Corporation sells a program called 'Music Maker' for use with its TI-499/A Home Computer. Much TI software for the Home Computer is cartridge-based solid state, but unlike the cartridge-type computers such as the Philips Videopac, the TI has full interface facilities to allow connection with either cassette or disk storage systems.

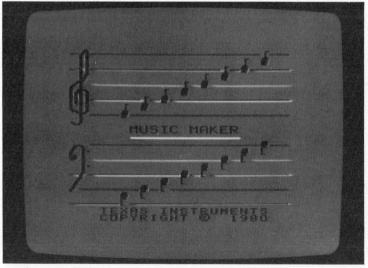

The screen display from the 'Music Maker' program which runs on the TI-499/A Home Computer. Two staves allow 'overdubs' to be created.

Music Maker is an excellent program offering the student three voices controlled by menu-driven software. As the TI Home Computer has full colour capability, considerable use is made of colour in guiding the novice. In the 'traditional mode' the student selects the note value from a range of notes shown at the side of the treble and bass clefs (whole note to sixteenth note) and then moves the cursor to the appropriate position on the staff. One measure at a time is completed with this program and at the end of a bar, the student may choose to go back and write a second and third voice in that bar before progressing to the next.

An important part of the Music Maker program is the 'Sound Graphs' sub-program. This is a method of music writing which abandons the traditional staves and allows novices to 'draw' their tunes on the screen, creating graphs which indicate the relative ascent and descent of the melody line. In the long term any serious student is likely to abandon this method of writing music, but the computer's graphics power is neatly harnessed to provide an interesting graphic representation of musical progression which will undoubtedly assist many people who have no understanding of conventionally written music. Unusually, the TI system allows for printed hard copy to be obtained from the screen display. Only TI's own Thermal Printer will work with the system, but several measures at a time may be printed if required.

The above programs are powerful teaching tools for children and adults, but the sounds produced are very limited, and serious teachers and musical-education establishments will require far better sound production from computers before they consider this technology to be a useful aid for intermediate or advanced musical tuition.

Several specialist manufacturers have developed advanced packages for musical tuition based on the use of popular small computers. Several of the packages described in Chapter 2, *The Personal Micro and Music* have educational applications, and some important teaching aids, developed especially for the purpose, have proved themselves successfully in universities and similar establishments.

Passport Designs of La Honda, California have produced several different software programs to run with their Soundchaser package. This package is described more fully in Chapter 2, but it basically consists of a musical type keyboard, printed circuit cards for sound production and software disks.

Their Music Tutor program requires the student or tutor to possess an Apple 48K computer with a disk drive system. To this is added Passport's own musical keyboard which is connected to the Apple's expansion bay on the 'mother board' inside the computer. One or two voice cards – providing an option of three or six voices – are also slotted into the internals of the Apple. Apple actively encourage owners to dig about in the insides of the computer, indeed, it is the only way many programs and packages may be connected.

The Passport Soundchaser system is available in two types: digital and analog. The first system includes digital cards produced by Mountain Computers and offers the user a digital method of sound production allowing waveforms and frequency envelopes to be created in the abstract. The analog system produces 'Moog synthesizer' type sounds from the hardware boards fitted to the computer and offers the user computer control over these. There are several software packages available for use with the Passport system, all of which are useful to the serious music student.

Dr Charles Boody of the University of Minnesota wrote the Music Tutor system. It is is designed for both the classroom and the home, and the four training units – Intervals, Matching & Tuning, Chords and Melodic Games – were designed to develop ear training as well as impart the basic principle of musical theory. The program incorporates drills which students can follow at their own pace. Each unit of the system has its own graphics display and the program provides encouragement and learning incentives, scoring, etc, to help the student assimilate the information. The program even has sufficient power and range to be of use to accomplished musicians. For example, chord drill questions students on the various inversions for chords, and complex counterpoints and harmonies are covered in the program.

A teachers' disk is supplied with the program and teachers can set up their own drills to correspond with the level of skill found in the class. Alternatively a teacher can use this disk to direct the program to concentrate on a particular subject area.

The analog cards in the system effectively turn the Apple into a synthesizer and for this reason the sounds produced are best described as 'electronic,' and are capable of considerable modification with filters, as in a conventional synthesizer.

An additional program which is very useful for tuition is Passport's 'Notewriter.' This program drives a standard dot-matrix printer to deliver monophonic printed music directly from musical keyboard input. This program allows the student to play music directly into the computer from the musical keyboard. The music is converted to conventional notation on the screen − all time values automatically sensed − and if the student wishes, this may be printed as hard copy by the printer.

In a classroom, a system such as the MusicTutor frees a teacher from repetitious drilling of the basics of music and allows a far greater amount of individual assistance. The total package of the Soundchaser system and software is presently not much more than $1,000 and with many schools already owning an Apple computer, such a program makes a useful contribution to a music syllabus.

Another Californian company, the Syntauri Corporation of Palo Alto, also markets a music package for use with the Apple. The software which is at the heart of the system was developed by Charles Kellner, one of Apple's own senior programmers, and Syntauri market his system which, like the Passport, has several software options.

The alphaSyntauri system is wholly digital. Using a digital oscillator produced by Mountain Computers, the package requires the user to insert a card into the Apple and then connect an organ-type keyboard to the computer. The system then runs on one of the several software systems sold by Syntauri. The whole system is described more fully in Chapter 2.

Syntauri call their music tuition program MusicMaster, and it is capable of taking the student from basics through to orchestration. A major emphasis in the program is on ear-training. Techniques for the development of this gift include the sounding of random notes which the student is required to identify, and chord identification.

Three levels make up the MusicMaster program: beginner, inter-mediate and advanced. The beginner module comprises an introduction to major, natural minor, harmonic and melodic minor scales and, in pursuit of their ear training philosophy, the authors of MusicMaster include recognition tests for scales which are played automatically. Alternatively students are required to play a scale as prompted by notation appearing on the video screen and to play scales from memory when the name of the scale appears. Interval tuition is developed similarly and basic triad chords, major, minor, augmented and diminished, are presented for recognition in both aural and written form.

The Intermediate and advanced modules cover such topics as rhythmic dictation, counterpoint and modulation.

Tutors may direct the program to concentrate on specific areas and built-in software scoring allows tutors and students to assess progress.

As a bonus to educational establishments, the program's designers, Dr Wolgand Kuhn (Stanford University) and Dr Paul Lorton (University of San Francisco), have incorporated administrative programs into the software which allow users to keep school, teacher and class files and which assist teachers in the preparation of reports. Facilities are embedded in the program to allow teachers to write their own sub-programs in order to analyze student performance.

The alphaSyntauri system with software but excluding the Apple II computer and peripherals is likely to cost between $4,000 and $5,000.

5 The Micro and the Percussionist

At first it seemed as though technology would replace the drummer – he would be the front-line casualty in a world of musical robots. 'A drummer only has to keep time and it's obvious that a well-programmed machine could do it better!' So the argument has run and although a classic music-business joke defines a band as three musicians and a drummer, nothing could be further from the truth. In the late 1960s, manufacturers produced the first rhythm boxes, but these were hardly a replacement for a drummer. For six or seven years the development of these devices remained static, mainly because they failed to become popular. This was hardly surprising – they sounded terrible! These early machines couldn't be programmed in the way we understand. A rotary control governed tempo and an assortment of bangs and clicks were delivered in various rhythm forms – waltz, rhumba, rock 1, rock 2, etc – with the accent placed variously, on *on* beats, *off* beats and often in between.

The sounds delivered weren't very convincing and only later models had any kind of drum break or fill built-in. The small popularity the drum boxes found was with electronic organists playing lounges which were unable or unwilling to afford a live drummer. It is possible that the unpleasant boom, chic, chic accompaniment that these boxes provided for organists was partly responsible for the wooden image most musicians now have of electronic home organs. By a process of natural evolution the drum boxes were absorbed into the organ itself and by 1972 most home and professional organs were available with built-in rhythm units.

During the 1970s home organs were a boom industry. Progress in micro-electronics allowed quite sophisticated instruments to be built inexpensively and ownership of an easy-play organ rapidly became a status symbol in 'executive' housing districts. Every shopping mall had its organ store and for a while the craze for automated music (very different to programmed music) threatened to lead the way. Other 'home entertainment' items such as video recorders, TV games, home computers, etc, have now replaced the organ/gadget box as a best-selling leisure product and the home organ has entered a rapid world-wide decline.

But the organ boom produced great advances in rhythm box design. By the end of the 1970s the rhythm sounds were, for the most part, very good – even cymbals being reproduced realistically. Usually the player could only call on a range of factory-set rhythms and sounds, selecting his tempo and mix of sounds, but he was able to accent the rhythm to his taste, almost mimicking a live drummer's performance.

Because of the development of the rhythm box, many cynics saw drum machines eventually taking over the drummer's role. Although the sort of boxes available in today's organs can substitute for a drummer, they can never replace him. But in 1979 came the first programmable rhythm machine.

The Japanese Roland Corporation is committed to applying semi-conductor technology to musical problems and they have often been the first into particular fields. In June 1979 they showed their 'Boss Doctor Rhythm' unit to the musical instrument trade at an exhibition in Chicago. I recall that the most interested people of all were the

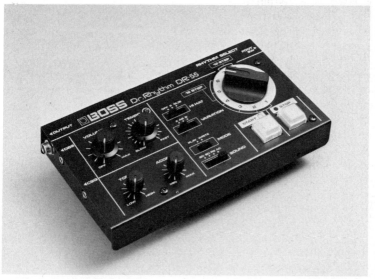

The Japanese Roland Corporation are well known as innovators of programm-able music machines. This 'Dr. Rhythm' by the Boss division of Roland was one of the first inexpensive programmable drum machines on the market.

drummers, not those who were seeking cost-effective replacements. Programmable music machines had been available previously — Roland had introduced the world's first computer music composer, the Roland MC-8 Micro-Composer in February 1977 — but never just for drums and never at $200!

The little box had a write switch which allowed the user access to the microprocessor memory. The user could record up to four simultaneous lines (bass drum, snare, hi-hat, accent), inputting each one individually. For example in a 4/4 signature the user could decide to have a bass drum beat on the 1st and 3rd beat of the bar. Each bar is separated into 16 segments in the microprocessor memory. The 'rest' button is used to indicate silence and so to place the bass drum on the 1st beat of the bar the user would press the play button once followed by seven rests, push the play button again to enter the bass drum on the 3rd beat and press the rest again seven times. In playback there would be just the bass drum sound on the 1st and 3rd beats. Moving the selector to the snare, the user might place this drum on the fifth and thirteenth segments of the memory corresponding with the 2nd and 4th beats in the bar. The other instruments could then be added at will. The division of the bar into 16 segments allows quite fine control over beat placing and complex rhythms may be built up. The machine replays the segment entered until stopped. An alternative memory location allows a second, independent, rhythm to be entered and during use the user can switch manually between the two rhythms or allow the machine to do so automatically.

In describing the use of this early programmable rhythm producer I have deliberately talked about 'the user.' In fact most purchasers and users turned out to be drummers or percussionists. They found the gadget particularly useful for tuition. They created drum breaks from their imagination, edited and changed them to establish the right effect and then learned to play them themselves. Few musicians who were not already drummers or percussionists could learn how to operate the programming even though they understood the time values involved. They could not imagine which combinations of bass drum, snare and hi-hat would sound right while the drummers knew from long experience, and were able to apply their knowledge and improve their own playing with the help of this small, limited device. Although still available, the Doctor Rhythm has become rather antiquated now. Many companies have developed products not only far more sophisticated but also *far easier to use and program*. Roland themselves now have far better versions which are also easier to program.

During 1981 and 1982 several drum computers were launched commercially. These gave the percussionist and the composer far greater control over programmed rhythms. Many music computers (and music software packages for personal home computers) were already available and capable of making very sophisticated drum sounds with complex programs, but the phrase 'drum computer' specifically refers to a dedicated computer which is packaged in such a way that a drummer or percussionist will quickly be able to work with it.

The advantage of such packaging will be obvious – very few drummers want to learn to operate a computer in order to play the drums (as yet). But there are also disadvantages; e.g. the computer can only be used for producing drum sounds. Although it possesses the capability to do so, it won't work out what you owe the tax man or let you play space games, as that would require a non-dedicated system.

The manufacturers have got it right, however, and in several instances have produced machines that are easy to use, *very* flexible in performance and which quickly stretch even seasoned performers and composers to their limits.

One of the first big machines was the LM-1 Drum Computer from the Linn Electronics Corporation of Los Angeles. This was first shown to the music industry in 1981. A year later the product had proved particularly successful in Great Britain – partly through the vigour of their UK distributors, Syco Systems – and at one point no less than six records in the British top ten had Linn Drums rather than live drummers. Artists making extensive use of the Linn include the Human League, Ultravox, Peter Gabriel, Dollar, ABC and Orchestral Manoeuvres in the Dark (see Chapter 10). In the summer of 1982 the Central London Branch of the Musicians' Union passed a resolution calling for a ban on Linn Drums and similar instruments from recording and broadcast sessions.

The main selling point of the Linn was that it offered real drum sounds; in fact recordings of drums that were stored digitally. This use of the micro put the Linn head and shoulders above old-style drum machines on sound quality alone – even before its advanced programmability was considered. The bass drum sound from a Linn was the sound of a superb bass drum recorded under ideal conditions. Its digital recording ensured that when the sound was redelivered it was *exactly* like the original bass drum. The same technique was used for recording the many other instrument sounds available in the Linn. The quality of sounds meant that record producers could get a great drum sound instantly in the studio. Drums have always proved difficult to record and the wasted hours of taping up drum heads became a thing of the past.

The criticism that drum sounds on record will all sound the same if Linns become widespread is fair. Indeed, British chart records have suffered from a monotony of rhythm sounds since Linn passed into regular studio use. The machine's independent sound outputs described below do allow producers to add a degree of individuality to the sounds, but it won't be until Linn users can record their own drums digitally into a Linn (a facility not far away) that the advantage of programmability will become available without the drawback of the constant re-use of standard sounds.

Despite the move made by the London branch of the Musicians' Union being akin to trying to stop the development of the internal combustion engine, the resolution caused short term difficulties. At a national level, the British Musicians' Union are still considering their position at the time of writing, but their cautious attitude conceals a Luddite feeling amongst some of the membership. In contrast, the AFM (American Federation of Musicians) have announced that the subject is 'no issue inside their organization'.

Labour worries are inextricably bound up with microprocessor advances and many agree that computers are the real cause of high unemployment in the developed world. Despite political soap-box stances calling for full employment, governments are now desperately wondering how best to break the news of permanent unemployment to generations previously taught that fulfillment in life depends on work.

The industrial revolution occurred when man learned how to reproduce and amplify his muscle, the information revolution has occurred because we can now amplify our minds. Being able to offer neither muscle or mind to the mechanized production of wealth, the working person without special skills is redundant. Some musicians are frightened that the application of artificial intelligence to music making will make them redundant. It is possible. One of London's best known session drummers suffered a drop in work of 60 per cent

The Linn Drum, LM-1. Along with the Fairlight CMI, the Linn Drum has the distinction of being one of the two most influential new musical instruments to appear in the last 20 years. This computerized drum machine has digitally recorded drum sounds stored within ROM and allows drummers to program even the most complicated drum parts. At one time, six records in the British top-ten featured Linn drums rather than human drummers and the London branch of the Musicians' Union called for a ban on such instruments.

between 1981 and 1982 – this was directly due to the introduction of drum computers. This player's main stock in trade was absolute reliability, a kit which could quickly sound good in a studio and his technical skill as a drummer. Lesser drummers can now program a Linn or another drum computer to perform this function.

At first glance the Linn, now in its second generation as 'The Linn Drum,' looks rather like a standard sound mixing console. The machine has 16 separate drum sounds: bass drum, hi-hat (open and closed), cabasa, tambourine, three tom-toms,two congas, cowbell, clave and hand claps, crash and ride cymbals, snare and side-stick snare – in fact every item you'd be likely to find in a good drum kit (and some you wouldn't). The 32 slide faders on the front panel that resemble a mixing console, mix the sounds together for the desired effect and these may be mixed whilst the machine is playing back. The drummer/percussionist can select his or her *own standard* of playing with this particular machine. He plays a rhythm into the machine, punching the button marked bass as he would kick his bass drum. There is a built-in fixed click which acts as both a metronome for the apprentice drummer and as a sync-pulse for a tape recorder and if his timing is still a little off, the machine will understand 'reading' the rest of his input what he's trying to do and will automatically correct it for him. Conversely for those who prefer a little random wander in their programs they can add human feel in the timing circuits which will add a controlled amount of erratic playing.

When the bass drum program has been written in, the snare may be written, then the hi-hat and so on. They may, of course, be written in any order. During play-back the relative levels of each sound may be controlled by the slide faders. The LM-1 offers a separate output for each sound which allows the individual signals to be sent separately to a mixing console where they can be 'treated' with equalisation, echo, etc if desired and panned separately to their stereo destinations.

I have not used the LM-1 or its cheaper and more sophisticated successor, the Linn Drum, (the LM-1 started at around $8,000, the Linn Drum is $4,000-$5,000!) but I can endorse the principle on which they have been designed. It contains many compromises but it is very user friendly — any drummer can write a complete part to a song; intro, first verse including breaks, choruses and ending, within an hour. This is the result of a good interface between the computer and the user. But in achieving this, some flexibility is sacrificed. It ought to be said here that the limitations I outline below are not peculiar to Linns — all current production drum computers have limitations of one kind or another, usually demanded for playing ease. Only when drummers/percussionists are prepared to learn another discipline, such as an input language for a computer or when speech input becomes available, will such limitations disappear.

Today's musician using the Linn and some others like it is limited to a certain memory capacity. In the case of the Linn it is 4,850 steps divided across 49 memories. Because of the way a computer stores information it is interested in the number of bits coming in, not how long they take. This means that to produce a song the part has to be cut into the sections to be entered into the 49 memories. The parts are the intro, fills, verses, solos, chorus, etc. After each section has been programmed and stored (each with up to 16 drums) the sections can be linked together in chains to form the complete song. Although this is a limitation, it works perfectly for structured and semi-structured music such as pop songs, rock, light music, etc, and it must be said that this would be the likely way of working even if the limitation didn't exist. Only in avant-garde and classical music does this limitation make the Linn's use impossible, but in these situations the accent is likely to be on the live performance and thus a pre-programmed drum part – even if the entire part could be entered as one – would be unlikely to be found acceptable.

A particularly useful feature is that complete programs may be dumped on to a high-quality cassette tape for storage. Thus memory space may be used for a particular number of songs and programs taken out of live memory and kept to be re-loaded again when necessary. Another very important feature of the Linn is a constantly live RAM. This means that when the mains power is turned off the memory does not forget the programs it holds. There are two ways for a machine to do this and if you're contemplating using a programmable instrument or computer which claims this feature, it is worth checking whether the RAM memory is supported during mains switch-off by a trickle charge of power from a small internal battery or whether the machine uses a more expensive 'bubble memory' for storage.

The bubble memory is a particularly valuable device principally developed by Texas Instruments at the end of the 1970s. This neat little memory stores the 1s and 0s in bubbles that, during access periods, move through the circuits. When shut-off occurs the bubbles cease to move, stay where they are and thus remember the last billion or so number strings. The reason for explaining all this is that bubble memory devices could become common in musical instruments (see the Prism keyboard in Chapter 7) in the near future.

Unfortunately bubble memory technology has suffered several set backs in the last few years. Texas pulled out of bubble memory development two years ago to be rapidly followed by another giant in the market, National Semi-Conductor. The reason for this abandonment lay more in a sudden lull in the semi-conductor market, which was hiccuping its way through a wild growth pattern, than in the technology. Several other giant corporations are still producing and supporting bubble memories and it now seems likely that the devices will, as originally predicted, take over much of the memory role from disks and other magnetic storage devices.

The advantage the bubble memory offers to musicians, militarists and space men is that it is rugged. Most computer applications take place in a nice, peaceful atmosphere – the living room, the studio, the laboratory, the school – but the world of the musician is a harsh and hostile place. Instruments which have to travel have to be rugged and there isn't an alternative storage system for computers which can be described as truly rugged. If the bubble memory resumes its growth curve, this robust and permanent memory system could well be found in many music products within a few years.

As well as the problems of magnetic memory storage, musicians also face small problems with the electrically-supported version of a RAM. If the tiny battery fails, you lose any program you are holding in RAM. For that reason it is always a good idea to use the dumping facility for every program you think you might like to keep – it uses very little tape space and cassettes are cheap. Here we come to a very important subject in computing: BACKUP.

As clever as computers are becoming they can always fail. Usually it is a failure of a mechanical component, the power supply, or human error – rarely the microprocessors themselves. When this happens you stand to lose a great deal of work if you haven't got backups of your programs. In computing, the rule is to work out how much creative time you can afford to lose – a day, half a day? – and whenever you are writing new programs you must make backup copies at that interval. If you follow this rule and the main fuse blows causing the whole program in RAM to die, you will have nearly everything copied. Failure to backup something important only happens to programmers once in their career.

The Linn Drum and its competitors offer far more control than I have described above. Digital recording allows very easy editing (enter the edit mode, playback, wait for the right place and play what you should have played first time) and the dynamics of the digital sounds can be altered to your taste. On most current drum computers this is the area in which you can do least. The main reason for this is that sound-shaping demands a huge amount of memory space – there is a great deal of information to analyse and store even in a single sound – and memory-space equals money. But the fundamental pre-set sounds themselves are excellent in most digital instruments I've heard.

A year or so after the first Linn appeared, Oberheim, the innovative US synthesizer company, introduced their drum computer, the DMX.

Oberheim's DMX drum machine has some similarities to the Linn Drum, but is part of an Oberheim family of programmable instruments. Drum sounds are recorded digitally and stored inside the DMX. Users can mix the balance of drums in the output section as well as take separate signals from each channel.

As a company already producing programmable synthesizers, they presented the machine as part of a programmable family and demonstrated this family system to the music industry at an important Atlanta music trade show in June 1982. The DMX boasts some momentary advantages over the Linn (momentary because technology is moving so fast) but also suffers by comparison in other areas. Like the Linn II, the DMX retails for a few thousand dollars. One of the DMX memory chips contains the digital recordings of actual acoustic drums; bass drum, six toms, two cymbals, snare, hi-hat and percussion. Obviously the user is stuck with the original sound as recorded by Oberheim, but as each drum voice has its own output, the individual sounds can be equalized to suit requirements. Bass drum and snare have three programmable volume levels to aid expression.

The micro memory in the DMX will store and recall 100 different rhythms and allows up to 50 drum parts for complete songs to be stored. A cassette output allows programs to be stored and re-loaded.

Like the Linn, if required, the DMX will guess what beat the user wanted to hit, even if the rhythm tapped out is a little woolly. When laying down a rhythm with the DMX, a metronome sound and a display read-out in beats per minute keep the player in line – one instance where automation may lead to a mechanical feel. Experienced players would probably prefer to record without this watchdog.

The memory capacity of the DMX isn't exhausted with these tasks. The machine will remember tempos set for each piece and reinstate the tempo control when a piece is called up out of memory for use. One of the most interesting features of the DMX is that each of the drum voices may be triggered from an external source. This means that a drummer can mike up his drum set (or practice pads), connect the mikes to an 'envelope follower' and in turn to the individual voice inputs on the rear of the DMX. The drummer can then play a drum part into the DMX instead of tapping the little buttons for input. This may offer experienced drummers a far more expressive way of entering the programs into the machine and it will certainly

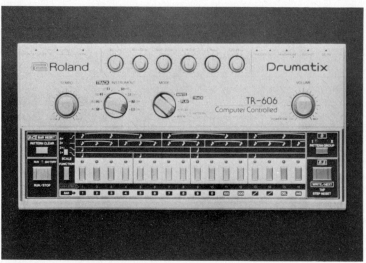

Today's Roland drum machines are highly sophisticated, like this TR-606. This machine allows the drummer to build rhythms bar by bar and then link the bars together to form complete sequences. The sounds currently produced by all Roland drum machines are analog.

help those drummers who insist that their best improvisations only come when the sweat is dripping from the tips of their noses. Naturally the DMX will provide a sync track for external sequencers, synthesizers and recording machines.

In the last few years there has been a flood of middle-range microprocessor-controlled rhythm machines arriving in the market place. Most of them are hybrids, using micros to remember the sequences entered but producing the sounds in synthesized analog form.

Typical of these are the excellent Roland rhythm machines which range in cost from a couple of hundred dollars to well over a thousand. These machines offer the players a set amount of memory, usually separated over several tracks. They are slightly harder to program than the fully digital machines and the player has to decide how long an individual measure is going to be before he starts entering. Typically the machines offer sounds similar to bass drum, snare, tom toms, cymbals, hi-hat and effects and all have a built-in battery to protect programs.

In the TR-808 Rhythm Composer the player is offered control over tuning, tone and decay on the individual voices and the 12 sound sources each have their own output allowing the voices to trigger external instruments. One could be used as a click track for example or be fed out to be individually panned by a mixer. LEDs and step switches assist the player in programming and a total of 768 measures can be memorized using all tracks. The tricks that belong to the old-style rhythm boxes remain on the TR-808, the automatic fills, etc, but the Roland machines offer an intelligent compromise in a rapidly shifting technology.

As in so many areas of life, the thoughtful musician may be tempted to enquire whether any purchase is sensible if development is occurring so quickly. 'Surely the thing I buy will be obsolete almost as soon as I have it?' is a cry that is frequently heard. The answer is simple. If you find an instrument or machine that will do what you want at a price you can afford, buy it! Undoubtedly a new product will soon appear offering more features for less money, but you must make a commitment and follow it through. The alternative is that you never get to grips with the new technology.

Interestingly, in all areas of microprocessor technology an ever larger software gap is opening up. This is not only a gap between the facilities of computer hardware and the ability of programmers to write programs that fully exploit its potential, it is also a gap between technology and human acceptance. People are not given time to assimilate and learn a new development in technology before they are being offered something new. It is a problem that Ikataro Kakehashi, the President of Roland considers serious:

'We must give people a chance to catch up. The two things that hold development up are the need to earn back the money it has taken to develop a product and the speed at which people can learn something new. The technology is available now for many new things.'

At the other end of the scale from the Linn and the DMX digital drum computers, Mattel the toy people and manufacturers of Intellivision the TV game/computer, shocked the musical world in 1982 when they entered the market place with a drum computer that had a retail price of around $200! This instrument was no toy, however, it was a fully fledged mini-version of the big drum computers and its features stunned the industry and musicians. It

The inexpensive Synsonics drum machine was one of the surprises of 1982. Produced by 'Mattel,' the toy company which also produces Intellivision, this little kit is fully programmable and offers tunable, digitally recorded drum sounds. The round rubber pads can be played with fingers or with drum sticks.

might have surprised them less had they known the quantum leaps that are occurring in micro development.

The Mattel Synsonics is a small, light instrument which has four rubber pads mounted on a flat surface. These pads may be hit with sticks as though they were normal drums (they are called snare, tom tom 1, tom-tom 2 and cymbal) and they are *pressure-sensitive*, they sound louder as you hit them harder. The bass drum is operated from a small rubber button on the control panel and there are three basic ways of playing the machine.

The machine will play like a conventional rhythm box: each of the five elements of the kit can be turned on to play at given intervals; the bass drum on the two 'on' beats in the bar, the snare drum on the two 'off' beats, the cymbal/hi-hat four beats and the tom-toms for fills. The tempo can be adjusted over a wide range by another of the rubber buttons. The pitch of the top tom-tom can be regulated over five octaves allowing it to sound like a second floor tom-tom or like the very high disco Syn-Drums. This control effectively offers the player several sounds out of the one pad.

The second, and most interesting, way of using the machine is in the recording mode. This mode is entered by pushing the record button on the small panel. The user then plays the pads with either sticks or fingers. The requirement for a drummer to adapt to hitting four small pads instead of large drums seems to cause less difficulty than would be imagined. The memory will hold up information across 16 down beats (eight 4/4 bars) and when the part is completed the player can listen back to what he has played. He can then adjust the tempo as he desires (without any pitch change taking place) and listen to his recording. In this way a difficult part may be entered slowly and played back at a faster speed. Obviously the machine will continue to repeat the entered program as a continuous rhythm until the player pushes the stop button.

During playback the player can edit the part, correcting missed beats or adding small fills. This alone comprises a powerful tool, but the Synsonics kit offers two more 16-beat memories which may be filled independently of the first. When parts have been entered into these, the three memories may be layered to make complex rhythm patterns. The first memory could contain the basic snare and bass rhythms, the second memory could hold tom-tom fills and the third the cymbal parts or alternatively they may be played in sequence. Playing them sequentially allows a player to plan his parts of a song

– as with the Linn. The first memory may hold the part to the verses, the second the chorus parts and the third the middle-8 section. Having filled the three memories, the player can then superimpose in those memories indefinitely building up a super-complex rhythm. This represents a fantastic cost/features ratio and is truly indicative of the power the micro is handing to the musician.

The third use for Synsonics is as a direct replacement for a drummer. The instrument can be used in real-time situations, but it is likely to be used mostly in studios as there is still the visual acceptability barrier to overcome for on-stage use. It has to be said that I have heard better drum sounds from other digital machines, but they are considerably more expensive.

As already mentioned, drummers and percussionists are the people benefiting most from the arrival of microprocessor drum machines. Pop music session drummers are now conferring with arrangers prior to the recording session, programming their total part, arriving at the studio and switching on their computer. They're still doing it in Britain despite the possible MU ban. The result has all of the feel the drummer would have delivered but is totally reliable (if the drummer's ill the computer can still make the session – if the computer's ill the drummer can always play!) and the producer knows how valuable 'first take' reliability is with recording time running at hundreds of dollars/pounds per hour.

This approach would probably not be acceptable to most musicians in a band situation, or where more serious music is to be made. The claim that the interaction between players would be lost is valid: many great recordings have relied on spontaneous changes made by the band during recording. However, it is surprising how many groups of musicians have begun to play together very happily with one (or more) of their members effectively a machine. (See Chapter 10, Warren Cann of Ultravox on the subject).

Another great benefit to be derived from the drum computer is its teaching power. This must not be confused with interactive teaching power in which a 'normal' screen computer takes over the role of the teacher and questions the student – although that facility will have a profound effect on musical education, see Chapter 4. The present generation of drum computers allows students to hear what they are trying to play, correcting as they go.

A typical drum lesson today might consist of half an hour behind a conventional drum kit and half an hour in front of the drum computer learning by trial and error the effectiveness of different time signatures and beat placings.

Obviously, the Synsonics is a powerful teaching tool and there can be few drum tuition studios unable to afford one or two. The use of the unit is so simple that it really does allows students to dissect their drumming as never before. I consider it likely that a good tutor-book and a Synsonics will offer as much to any novice as the second-rate percussion tuition available in many small towns.

Tuned percussion lends itself to computer control. Fewer intelligent products are available for the tuned percussionist than for the drummer, but those that are have begun to harness considerable power.

In tuned percussion the player is combining two disciplines – rhythm and melody. Of course, all musicians do this to a greater or lesser extent but in the percussionist the two are equally important. The use of mallets, hammers, beaters, etc to create musical tones is important in rhythmic precision and speed, and although perfectly true vibe and chime sounds etc can now be produced by other instruments, by keyboard-controlled digital synthesizers for example, keyboard players are unlikely to give the right feel to a vibes passage and vibes players aren't able (or willing) to learn keyboard technique. The problem is solved by the 'tuned-percussion computer.'

At the time of writing there are at least two such instruments commercially available and by the time you read this I'm sure there will be many more. The first to be produced was the Synare MP (Mallet Percussion) built by Star Instruments Inc. of Stafford Springs, Connecticut. This was first shown to the industry in June 1981 and it resembled an oversized vibraphone housed in a metal cabinet.

Instead of metal tone bars each bar is a rubber pad which may be struck with conventional sticks, mallets, beaters, etc. The scale of the bar layout is slightly wider than in a conventional vibe or mirimba but this is to facilitate ease of playing and as the keyboard is both transposable and expandable, no playing scope is sacrificed.

The instrument is a marriage of digital and analog technology and the sounds produced are varied and include conventional vibe, xylophone and mirimba effects. These sounds are made by conventional voltage-controlled oscillators. These sounds are very good indeed although soon there will be a tuned percussion computer that creates all the tones digitally and thus creates the actual sounds rather than synthesized sounds. The distinction is a very slim one, especially when made against such an instrument as the Synare, but it should be made.

The microprocessor part of the instrument enables it to record up to six overlaid sequences, each comprising up to 240 notes. As with the Linn and DMX drum computers, these shortish sections can be 'chained' together to make full song baselines or complete parts, although the Synare MP doesn't have quite the same flexibility as the Linn for sequence variation. Consequently the recording facility is most likely to be used for listening to how a particular sequence sounds during rehearsal, or for writing repetitive themes which appear under the main melody. Nevertheless, it is a very powerful instrument.

Because the memory is digital, total editing control is theoretically possible but, as with many performance instruments at present, the flexibility has not been fully exploited. Whilst watching a Synare MP demonstrated to a group of percussionists I was astonished by *their* astonishment, but it must be a shock for a fifty-year-old professional vibes player to discover a set of vibes that sound good, offer four octaves (with the ability to take more), which can remember and replay perfectly the sequence that has just been played whilst allowing instant key transposition during replay – is polyphonic with 4-note chord ability and which *costs no more than an average set of traditional vibes!*

For the simple reason that there are far more drummers than tuned percussionists, the drummers have attracted the most attention from the instrument makers. Tuned percussionists still do not have the same computer power over their chosen method of making music – although they can benefit from more fundamental computer music control outlined in other chapters. But before long every drummer will be able to tune the drums of a drum computer to any pitch he chooses. Then drummers will become tuned percussionists almost by accident.

The expensive Fairlight dedicated music computer described in Chapter 9 has recently added a facility which effectively places tuned percussion under computer control. The new 'Page R' software development allows musicians to create rhythms and/or melodies step by step in real-time in a manner not dissimilar to the method of programming a Linn Drum. The advantage of this far more powerful instrument is that any sound may be used in rhythm and any pitch assigned to individual notes. A fuller explanation appears under the Fairlight heading.

The drummer and the tuned percussionist will benefit as much as other musicians from the microprocessor. Because of the enormous physical release drumming offers, I suspect that the desire to hit drums hard and rhythmically will continue unabated, but whether those drums will remain purely acoustic is doubtful.

6 The Micro in Performance

The moment you step out on stage you are alone. It is a fundamental truth which every seasoned performer knows. Take the micro with you, and the odds shorten in your favour.

Micro-assistance for musical performance first became available in the middle 1970s. A London company, EMS, produced several programmable analog instruments but the major marketing break-through came in 1977 when a Californian company, Sequential Circuits, produced a synthesizer capable of remembering 'patches' that had been set-up beforehand. It could even remember tunes and sequences loaded before the performance.

With this tool, keyboard players could step on stage knowing that their instrument could be set up perfectly at the touch of a button and that, if they chose, the keyboard intro to the first number could be played from the keyboard memory – a safe way of getting into the performance. How many sets have you heard in recent years which have started with a string of notes that seem to come from nowhere?

The Prophet synthesizer from Sequential Circuits was not the world's first micro-aided instrument, but it was certainly the first to combine the micro with an analog synthesizer is such a way that musicians found it both easy to use and extremely powerful. Not surprisingly, it sold like hot cakes.

The micro has entered into many diverse musical fields. It is an obvious element in the rare performances of quasi-classical 'Music Concrete' electronic music, but it also supports bands like the Human League, Toto, Depeche Mode and Orchestral Manoeuvres in the Dark in their stage acts. The ultimate users are Kraftwerk who take their electronics laboratory on stage and use it as a set. But to an extent, Kraftwerk and their like are the exception that proves the rule. Producing music that sounds electronic is not the final applica-tion of the microprocessor. The device is capable of much more. The English synthesizer bands are currently leading the world in the use of micro-synthesizers as replacements for conventional instruments and a typical set by the Human League or Depeche Mode features no acoustic/electric instruments or back line amplification at all.

Quite why British bands have taken the lead in musical fashion is unclear. In keeping with the nihilistic attitude which rules the popular-music segment of the business, the musicians insist that they use computer instruments because they can't play well enough to use conventional instruments. This attitude has its roots in the punk movement which started in Britain in 1975 and stated as its fundamental musical/political theme that experience and musicianship were unimportant: all that was relevant was youth, energy, the clothes you wore and the right kind of disadvantaged background. While British youth threw its highly skilled 'old guard' of musicians to the wolves, America continued to build on the concept that the better the band the better for everybody. Subsequently, rock-music growth-patterns in the two countries diverged, leaving American bands to push their musicianship to the limits and British punk musicians to concentrate on clothes, image and the peripherals of the video/computer/unemployed society.

The end result was not unhealthy for British music although for a time many observers despaired at the seeming decline in the musical standard of the successful new bands in Britain. In the late 1970s this reached an all time low as may be seen by the confused and directionless state of the record charts of the period. But from the ranks of this new wave, emerged a handful of songwriters and songcreators who owed no allegiance to past traditions in rock and who found new methods of creating music.

It is this emotional break with music created before 1975 that opened the door for such rapid assimilation of the inverse musical disciplines of microprocessor music. In general, American rock staggers on with the burden of 30 years of musical history on its shoulders. In Britain there are no respected historical voices to slow progress down.

Critics point to the lifelessness of the music made by the British electronic bands and much of this criticism is accurate. But remember that the music is still in the experimental stage.

Ian Craig Marsh who is a former member of the Human League and is now behind Heaven 17, the British Electric Foundation and other projects, is a prime example. It is natural for him to program the music he is going to record or perform and only now is he discovering the possibilities that acoustic instruments offer. But his approach specifies them as being peripheral to his programmed musical core.

This attitude is only the beginning of a new concept of music making in which, for many, the idea of playing an instrument live will be inconceivable. In live performances the concentration will be on the show, the clothes, the singing, the dancing, the special effects and audience contact. Most of the music played during the performance will have been recorded at a different time and place. This is the nature of 'pop' where the audience reacts as much to the individual images of the people involved as to the music.

In America, mainstream pop may well ingest the microprocessor effortlessly, applying it to the quest for better music without any deviation from this goal.

As suggested in Chapter 1, one possibility is that the public may react to the increasing trend towards pre-programmed music by placing special value on an artist's live performances.

Whatever effect the microprocessor has on musical presentation in the short to medium-term future, it also offers the conventional musician considerable power in ways other than pure musical control. Several microprocessor-controlled mixing desks and lighting-control systems are now available and these offer phenomenal control opportunities.

One of the first mixers with microprocessor power suitable for PA use was the DM Series Multi-track Console from the British company PACE. As may be guessed from its name, the desk was designed for use for both live and studio applications, but the way in which the microprocessor was originally applied made it particularly flexible when used with PA systems used by touring bands.

The mixer was introduced in the summer of 1981 and although its format (20 into 4 or 8) wasn't unusual, a microprocessor module was installed that allowed the engineer complete control over routing. This auto-patch system switched individual inputs, via solid-state switches to any chosen pair of output faders. At first this may not seem a significant step forward, but consider a band on tour. The micro memory holds 16 factory pre-set routing combinations that can be re-called by a pre-set button and the system allows for 128 different routings in every single patch.

During a set an engineer may well face a main mix (all the band plus vocals) with, perhaps, a front-line-mike mix for an acoustic segment, a mix of drum mikes only for a five minute drum solo, and then a vocal-mike-only mix for a harmony piece. With conventional mixers each change demands all unwanted faders to be brought down and restored at the next change – not easy in a dark concert hall, as the feedback howls so often testify. With the DM desk (and undoubtedly with the others that will follow) each of these combinations can be held in memory. Thus at the beginning of the performance the LED display indicates that patch 1 is in use offering all channels for instruments and vocals to the appropriate outputs. When the acoustic segment arrives the engineer merely punches number 2 on the calculator-type keypad in the console and the unwanted channels are automatically cut out and the channels for the acoustic segment are routed as was previously planned. At the end of the acoustic segment, the engineer punches 1 back in again until it is time for the drum solo and so on. This type of automation leaves the engineer free to concentrate on the balance of the faders in use at the time. A scratch pad is provided below the micro control buttons for the engineer to note which patch is for which configuration.

In a recording situation the routing system merely offers a saving in time and is less advantageous, but when used as a 'drop-in' tool it allows silent drop-ins to be made by punching up the different patch at the appropriate moment.

The DM desk is built with a bus – a connector circuit – which allows the intelligent part of the desk to expand. PACE say their plan is to introduce subsequent software for the desk which will allow micro control over all of the desk's functions (including mixing) and an interface system which will allow settings to be saved on cassette or floppy disk. Consideration is also being given to the introduction of micro-controlled stage lighting from the desk.

The small automated mixing desks that are just appearing on the market aren't really suitable for live applications, but add-on units such as the Roland CPE-800 Compu-Editor can be useful both for sound and lighting.

Of course, lighting is an obvious contender for micro-control, although the subject really falls outside the scope of this book. A micro is useful when anything of a repetitive nature is undertaken and many light shows are repetitive. As music performances move further on to the programmed plane, so co-ordinated lighting may be controlled by a microprocessor taking its time from the basic click-track that is controlling the tempo of the performance. This will mean that quite complex light changes will always occur on cue and the days of the spotlight failing to pick out the soloist will be gone forever.

Manufacturers are confused by the micro revolution. They are currently approaching musicians from several standpoints – as the headings to the chapters in this book will reveal. Many of the established instrument manufacturers such as Yamaha and Moog believe that the musician wants a musical instrument that utilizes micro power as a feature within an instrument which looks and feels like a conventional keyboard. On the other hand, computer companies are convinced that the power of the stand alone microcomputer is sufficient attraction to enable them to market musical packages. These packages are unwieldy compared to stage-type keyboards, but they are usually more powerful. Some manufacturers, mostly those new to making musical instruments, have developed hybrid machines which have the appearance of a conventional keyboard coupled with some of the features of a stand alone computer (as in Chapter 2.) Of course there are also the large, dedicated music computers described in Chapter 9, but these are expensive and are likely to become performance tools only for the most successful musicians.

The instruments described in this chapter are made principally by the conventional musical instrument manufacturers who obviously have the performing musician in mind. But most of the instruments described in the hybrid section are also well-suited to performance and they are separated merely by the different philosophy that lies behind their design.

Most of the major manufacturers seem to think that a musician is either unwilling or unable to get to grips with even the simplest elements of computer technology. The idea of producing an instrument which uses floppy disks as a storage medium appears uncommercial and the manufacturers are developing ways of interfacing the musician and the micro which demand minimal learning from the player.

Some of these instruments are highly successful, but they all fail to make the best use of the micro power at their disposal and few are flexible enough to allow software updating as new developments arrive.

One exception is the Prophet, the first really successful programmable synth. Untypically, this performance-oriented instrument comes from a company with no tradition of musical instrument manufacture. In fairness, it should be pointed out that, despite my classification of the instrument as a performing tool, the instrument is highly versatile and has been heard on many hits. My categorization of it as a performance instrument principally acknowledges its compact, user-friendly design.

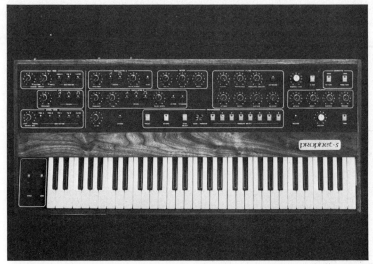

Getting the microprocessor to perform flexibly on stage was a challenge, and one of the companys which met it most successfully was Sequential Circuits who produced the Prophet Range of computer-assisted synthesizers in 1978. The Prophet 5 and 10 have become one of the most successful synthesizer ranges ever produced and are now available in third generation form.

Since 1981 Prophets have been built to a design which allows constant retrospective updating as new software and peripheral items become available. Such an attitude is anathema to some traditional companies who view this year's feature as a selling aid, and next year's feature as an inducement to replace. But the attitude of up-ratable products is one that has a firm hold in the computer world and this dichotomy of marketing attitude emphasizes the confusion the micro has caused in the musical instrument industry.

Sequential Circuits was set up in 1976 and the first Prophets were produced in January 1977. These were the first synthesizers to make use of a microprocessor that has since become almost universal – the Z-80. This 8-bit computer-on-a-chip is now at the heart of the majority of home computers (including the Sinclair ZX81) and many musical instruments.

The two instruments first launched were the Prophet 5 and 10, offering five and ten voices respectively. The original Prophet 10 was quickly withdrawn due to design faults, but the Prophet 5 took the synthesizer world by storm.

A new version of the 10 was delivered a year or so later and since then both synthesizers have been constantly revised. The more popular Prophet 5 has been through five up-dates at the time of writing. There was a complete redesign at update three (called Revision 3 by Sequential) and the subsequent versions are called 3.1., 3.2. and so on. It is the series 3 instruments that are capable of accepting the new software updates.

The Prophets are basically analog synths similar to Moogs, Korgs, etc but which have been placed under computer control. Each of the voices may be shaped as desired using the familiar control approaches offered by government of the oscillators, filters and envelope shapes (ADSR). On analog synths it is often very difficult to recall the exact settings that produced a particular sound. On the Prophets, these patches may be recorded in the micro memory and recalled at will. The individual controls do not require manipulation — their output is as the patch demands, no matter where they are placed physically. The Prophet 5 is supplied with 40 patches pre-programmed — brass, strings, organ, electronic pianos, etc — and the user can modify or replace any of these patches.

A normal sequence of operation with this analog/digital hybrid instrument is as follows: the player switches on the instrument and decides what sound is desired for the piece of music to be played. The player then selects one of the 120 patches that exist in the 15 memory banks and this is instantly loaded into the instrument. He or she can then play the keyboard to hear the sound of the patch and modify it accordingly. If the modified sound is preferred, the player can either a) replace the pre-set patch with the modified patch, or b) save the modified patch as a program separate from the original patch.

This facility offers tremendous advantages on stage when each number is likely to require different sounds from the synthesizer. Between each number the player has only to punch up the programmed patch required. At heart the Prophet is still an analog synthesizer, better suited to making synth-type sounds than attempting to duplicate strings or brass — to do this properly demands digital recording and storage of these sounds.

An interesting and useful feature on later Prophets is the computer tuning system. As most synth players will know, analog oscillators have a nasty tendency to drift out of tune, and the microprocessor in the Prophet has been programmed to check all of the oscillators in the instrument and correct wayward voltages. This operation is completed in a few seconds. During performance, the player can ask the microprocessor to check tuning again and the instrument control panel will 'go down' for a few seconds while this is done. When tuning is complete, the LEDs come on again.

Control over tuning is yet another way in which the arrival of the microprocessor is going to change the whole nature of music. The program in the Prophet's micro allows the oscillators to be tuned in scales other than the conventional equal-tempered scale.

This is not the place for a discussion on the merits of various tuning scales, but it is worth mentioning that the half-tone intervals we are familiar with – as found in all pianos, organs etc – are a tuning compromise arrived at to enable the instrument to be played reasonably satisfactorily in all keys. This method sets all the steps between semitones equal and is thus called the equal-tempered scale. If an instrument can be completely retuned for different keys – as the Prophet can – then a far more accurate scale system may be used. Such a scale exists – it is called the just scale, and it is both more accurate and more pleasing to the ear. This scale has the relative notes in the octave more accurately positioned in relation to the root note, particularly the fifth and the third, but the step sizes are unequal which makes playing in a key other than the one tuned for, very difficult – unless a player can instantly retune.

The equal-tempered scale is, in fact, out of tune for much of the time. On the Prophet – and many other computer-based instruments – this long endured anomaly can be corrected.

The 120 memory banks in the Prophet can be used for storing either patch programs or musical scales – only one scale or patch can be stored in any one memory at one time. Twelve of the front panel rotary controls on the instrument alter their function when the 'Scale Mode' is selected: they become rotary tuning pots for the twelve notes of the octave: C to B. Their marked function is disconnected while in the Scale Mode and Sequential Circuits supply adhesive labels to identify the controls whilst they are involved in tuning. Using these controls, the player can retune the notes of the octave to the just scale using any root note appropriate. In this way a tuning for each key may be stored in separate memory locations and recalled at the touch of button. The rotary controls offer tuning ability of one tone above the note and a half tone below the note.

As several other digital and digitally controlled synths have this ability, it obviously suggests that a growing amount of music is going to be in the just scale – a step which even those cynical about computers and music cannot decry. It is also possible for the player to experiment with tunings other than those conventionally accepted and so develop new musical structures.

As a result of their pioneering work, Sequential have secured themselves a sizeable chunk of the synthesizer market. The Prophet 10 (essentially two 5s banked together) has been successfully re-introduced; and the addition of optional polyphonic digital sequencers turns the Prophets into flexible recording machines.

Sequencers were one of the first digital gadgets to arrive in the musical marketplace. No musician could have been left unaware of their power after hearing The Who's *Who's Next* album and sequencers have rapidly become an accepted part of musical hardware.

Sequencers are digital stores of electrical information (not of numerically expressed sound, as in digital recorders). The notes in a synthesizer are triggered by electrical impulses sent by the keys. Sequencers store these impulses and redeliver them as requested. Tempo can often be altered, but usually none of the real control over important elements such as pitch, dynamics or editing is to be found. The exception to the rule is the clever family of sequencers produced by Roland years ahead of other manufacturers. The MicroComposers, the MC8 and MC4, described in Chapter 8, store electrical trigger information rather than sound and ought really to be considered sequencers, although they offer complete control over many aspects of music.

Other manufacturers were not slow to follow Sequential's lead and today there is a wide variety of digital/analog and completely digital machines on the market designed primarily for performers.

The Jupiter-8 from Roland follows the same concept of digital control for an analog synthesizer, but more automatic features – such as automatic arpeggios – are built in. The instrument is eight-voice polyphonic and has 64 user programmable memories – significantly less than the Prophets.

Great keyboard versatility allows the player to split up the keyboard and have one patch assigned to the top end and another to the bottom. The auto arpeggiator may then be used to create arpeggios on the bottom half of the keyboard (taking one root note from the player) while the player adds polyphonic chords or effects on the upper half of the keyboard. Additionally the keyboard may be operated in a dual mode – controlling two patches – essentially putting two separate sounds under each key. There are several other ways of using the keyboard and the amount of control over the 12 oscillators is impressive. An LED readout provides information about the patch currently in use and connections for off-loading memory information on to cassette are provided on the back panel.

There are several other digitally-controlled analog synths on the market. Many have the ability to save programs on cassette and all offer a degree of control over tone production that has been sorely needed. The great advantage these keyboards have over wholly digital synthesizers is price. The most elaborate digital/analog instrument is about the same price as the least sophisticated digital instrument. But that is likely to change within the next few years.

Each manufacturer views the musician and the marketplace differently, and the divergence of attitudes mentioned earlier is illustrated by Yamaha's response. This Japanese company is anxious that the arrival of digital technology shouldn't require the musician to have any degree of technical or programming knowledge. In producing the GS1 and GS2 digital performance-oriented instruments, they have produced keyboards which seem simpler to use than a standard synthesizer yet offer a wider range of sounds than would be possible with any analog/digital combination. The voices are produced digitally and memory capacity allows 16 voices to be held at one time. Yamaha have created a storage system using magnetized cards inserted into a slot adjacent to the keyboard to load sounds into the memories. Yamaha claim that they have created a vast library of sounds for the musician to choose from and presumably this will be added to.

Undoubtedly these instruments offer the performing musician far more variety of sound than has been available before, but once a sound is digitally stored, the control possibilities become almost infinite. These instruments could be capable of recording sequences and interfacing with external computers (admittedly at extra cost) but Yamaha seem to consider such options unimportant. Their development of a storage system unique to Yamaha indicates a desire to ignore the potential benefits of interface with external computers or even exchange of information (voices, etc). This may stem from a profound belief that the 'real' musician will want little to do with computer technology, or it could come from a commercial desire to ensure that new voices for the instruments have to be purchased from Yamaha.

In fairness it must be said that Yamaha have a fine tradition in instrument building. The instruments mentioned are of the finest quality and capable of satisfying the most demanding classical or rock musician, but in an attempt to make their instruments user-friendly and suitable for the non-technical musician, Yamaha, like several other companies, are denying access to many useful micro

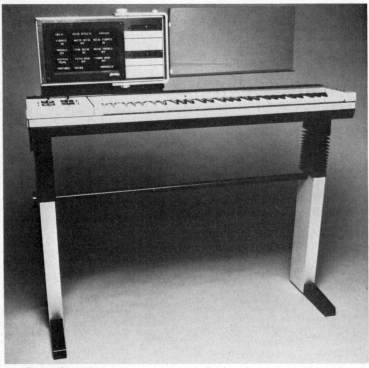

The Synthia. This music computer is wholly digital and powerful enough to be classed as 'dedicated', but it is entirely performance-oriented in design. Control is achieved via a touch-sensitive VDU and a large number of analog-type keyboard controls offer the player expression over sound.

facilities. It is a choice between ease of use and lack of control that only the musician can make.

Some companies attempt to find a new route between making an instrument suitable for 'unintelligent musicians' whilst also offering a real slice of computer power. The Synthia, produced by Adaptive Systems Inc. in Delaware, a company new to musical instrument manufacture, is such a system. The package has significantly less power than some of the dedicated instruments described in Chapter 9, but in many ways qualifies for consideration in this group rather than as a medium-priced performance keyboard. Its price is around $10,000.

This instrument is controlled from a touch-sensitive visual display

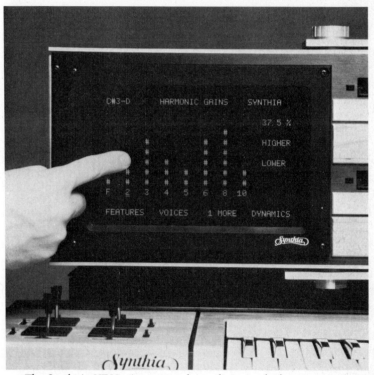

The Synthia's VDU. A musician has only to touch the screen to issue a command to the Synthia's processor.

screen. Menu options are displayed on this screen and the musician has only to touch the selection of his choice and the command is carried out. The screen is mounted on top of a musical keyboard and there is no alphanumeric keyboard.

Four joysticks are provided on the Synthia's keyboard and some treatments are pre-programmed rather than user programmable. Such treatments include randomness which supposedly increases the realism of synthesized instruments. The design philosophy behind the Synthia seems to concentrate on the reproduction of conventional instrument voices in a performance package. Odd assignments are possible – putting a saxophone at the lower end of the keyboard and a violin at the top provides a keyboard spectrum in which an ascending scale changes from a saxophone to a violin in gradual stages.

The Synthia is very easy to use and requires little of the study demanded by the home-computer based systems or the dedicated music computers.

Some of the best-known names in performance instruments are also coming up with packages that offer micro-power in a performance configuration. Rhodes, the CBS-owned maker of the popular Rhodes piano, have opted for simplicity in design and have striven to find compatability with musicians in their own way. The new Chroma synthesizer is based on a mechanical action keyboard which is closer to a piano action than an electronic keyboard. The instrument is a digitally-controlled analog synthesizer which offers later adaptions of the 'housekeeping' systems which Sequential Circuits introduced with their Prophets. One important additional feature on the Chroma is the provision of an RS-232 interface socket. This socket is the standard interface system for the computer industry and it allows the Chroma to connect directly with personal computers. CBS have developed software to run on Apple and TRS-80 computers and the addition of these systems will allow massive, multi-layered, sequences to be recorded and a great number of patches to be stored and recalled. This approach to musicians makes good sense. On the one hand the musician's technique is respected by the incorporation of a fully dynamic, mechanical keyboard backed up by circuitry that can interpret the nuances of that technique. On the other hand, the players intelligence is respected and facilities are provided which allow communication between intelligent machines.

Any well-stocked music store will be able to show a performance-oriented musician a large number of analog/digital and digital performance keyboards. The selection of the right one depends entirely upon the musician's needs and ability to deal with technical complexity. Compatability should be an important consideration and whether a keyboard will interface with other keyboards and with a computer (for greatly enhanced control) should be considered when making the final choice.

7 The Micro/Instrument Hybrids

Manufacturers of electronic musical instruments are adapting to the challenge of the microprocessor in different ways. To some extent, companies are governed by their traditions and whilst companies such as Yamaha, with long-standing instrument-making traditions, are building microprocessor instruments which differ little in appearance from conventional instruments, new companies, especially those with no instrument-building traditions, are adopting radically different approaches.

The application of the micro to music has pulled a number of new companies into the marketplace, many of them with origins in computing rather than music. This has lead to a confusion in technological ideologies: certainly, it has lead to a profusion of widely different instruments being available.

At one extreme, traditionalists believe that musicians won't happily learn computing techniques while, at the other extreme, companies like Fairlight in Australia believe that the power the micro has to offer will be enough to motivate musicians to learn some basic computing discipline. To some extent all this depends on whether the manufacturer is aiming for the minority or the mass market. Somewhere in between is the domain of the hybrid.

In the last few years a group of musical instruments has been launched which is a cross-bred group, in which computer and musical-instrument technology is mixed. The aim is to produce instruments which will appeal to performing musicians whilst making the best use of micro power. There is little doubt that once good musical systems are attached to personal computers they become musical instruments but they have poor mobility – despite manufacturers' claims to the contrary. The big dedicated computers, described in Chapter 9, *can* be packed and moved for road use but they are expensive and are an overkill solution for the average club gig. In the last few years a new species of instrument, free-standing with a disk drive at one end and a musical keyboard at the other, has evolved and these form the new generation of instruments, best described as hybrids.

One of the first hybrids was shown to the musical instrument trade for the first time at a trade show in Chicago in June 1981. Called the Emulator, this relatively inexpensive instrument combined a keyboard, a computer and a disk drive to offer a fully programmable, portable digital synthesizer.

The Emulator has been successful and it is now being made with development modifications. The company behind the Emulator are Eµ (pronounced Emu) Systems of Santa Cruz, California, a company established in 1972 originally to produce high-quality modular analog synthesizers. The man behind Emu is Dave Rosum, a scientist with a background in biochemistry. The modular synthesizers produced are very expensive and sell in small numbers to recording studios, educational establishments and similar. Flagship of this range is a digital/analog combination called the Audity which has a price tag of around $70,000.

The story of the Emulator is one of design skill overcoming

Half computer, half musical instrument, the Emulator has been one of the most successful of the 'hybrid' musical instruments. Sounds are loaded into the instrument by floppy disk, which is inserted into the slot to the left of the keyboard. Sequences may be stored and edited, but many performance controls are also provided.

economics. Despite the relatively small amount of computing power provided by the popular Z80 chip – 128K RAM compared to the 200+RAM of the bigger dedicated computers—Emu have managed to achieve some significant control.

The user loads sound into the Emulator from $5\frac{1}{4}$ in. disks. The disk drive slot is located to the left of the single musical keyboard. The disk drive system fitted to the instrument is very powerful and this loads 60K into RAM in just a few seconds. Mechanical components are usually the least reliable part of computer technology, but reports indicate that the disk drive system used in the Emulator is tough enough for constant use on the road.

Emu supply a wide range of disks with sounds already recorded (two per disk) and these two sounds are loaded, making the instrument ready to play. The four octave keyboard may be split, allowing a different sound to appear on the lower and upper halves of the keyboard, or it may be played with one sound under all the keys.

The sounds supplied on the Emu disks have been recorded digitally and may be reproduced at any pitch. The sample length in the Emu is limited to two seconds, and sustain is achieved by looping the sample. This technique prohibits absolute fidelity in reproduction of long sounds – piano for example – but produces an equivalent so close few would notice the difference under amplified conditions.

Using the disks available from Emu, the Emulator may sound precisely like a wide variety of conventional instruments. How close the simulation can be, depends more on the keyboard player's skill in mimicking the playing *style* of the instrument, than on the sound available.

The real power of the Emulator is revealed when the user records sounds of his own. Inputs are provided for both mike and line and the user may sample any type of sound – from an electric guitar to a sparrow. For example: using a good-quality microphone, one note of a trumpet may be recorded – perhaps middle c. This sound is sampled by the Emulator and stored in RAM. The player may press C above middle C and the trumpet sound is reproduced at that pitch, or any other note held down by the player. The keyboard is eight note polyphonic and thus a chord of trumpets may be played. As mentioned, long sustained notes are made possible by the looping system.

This technique may be applied to any sound – dog barks, train whistles, and every conventional instrument. Sampled sounds may be saved on a disk for later recall.

The price of the Emulator (less than half that of the dedicated computers) does force certain compromises. One of these occurs in the sampling rate, which is fixed at 30Hz producing a bandwidth limited to 10k. This bandwidth seriously limits the fidelity of certain sounds but although the ADC and DAC are only 8-bit, quantization noise is kept down to a respectable -72dB. For a fuller description of these problematic areas, see Chapter 9. The inevitable, unavoidable jargon is explained in the Glossary.

When sampling resonant sounds like a human voice or a grand piano, the single-sample technique isn't quite good enough. Although the Emulator will quite happily sample one note from a grand piano and reproduce it at any pitch required, it won't sound very realistic as the selected pitch moves away from the sampled pitch. The reason is that the harmonic and amplitude envelopes change, in addition to the pitch, in natural acoustics and no information on this is available in the single-sample technique. Emu say that the effect on a voice is not that of a voice changing pitch, but of bigger or smaller people singing.

To combat this, Emu offers users an optional disk containing software which converts the system into a multi-sampling system. This allows the user to sample sounds up to eight times across the four octaves under the keyboard, depending on available RAM. Thus a grand piano may be sampled eight times across the keyboard and the samples assigned to the correct parts of the Emulator's keyboard. In playing, the Emulator will use the nearest sample for information and thus closer duplication of resonant instruments are made possible.

The designers of this hybrid have made sure that performance controls are provided to govern the sounds produced. Pitch bend (real-time), vibrato and filters are provided and foot pedals assist in the control operations.

The Emulator is fitted with a powerful digital sequencer. Nine-hundred notes may be stored and full overdubbing and editing facilities exist; effectively offering the player a multi-track digital tape recorder — the only limitation being the number of voices the Emulator can sound at once during replay (2,4 or 8 depending on which version of the Emulator has been purchased). All sequences may be stored on disk with all relevant information about voices and timing embedded.

Emu offers a substantial array of support items in addition to the multi-sample software. Interface problems are taken seriously by the company and the Emulator owner may add an RS-232 port (Emus communicating down phone lines!) as an analog interface allowing a second means of communication with analog machines – the first is the sampling system. Other connections include a personal computer interface and a sequencer sync interface. As each disk holds only two sounds, it is likely that the keen sound creator will rapidly fill up disks. Standard $5\frac{1}{4}$ in. disks may not be used in the Emulator as the track format used on the disk is peculiar to Emu. Out of the goodness of their hearts, Emu will, however, sell the user an item of software which will allow regular disks to be formatted on the spot. This program costs several hundred dollars! Emu publish a library of programmed sounds from which the user may choose new sounds to add to the 20 sounds provided in the basic cost of the instrument. In many respects, the Emulator represents a superb combination of value, technology and musical qualities. Emulator systems are priced between $6,500 and $10,000.

In using a floppy disk storage system, Emu have clearly stated their close relationship with micro-computers: Crumar, on the other hand, have tried to develop a wholly digital synthesizer that spurns its antecedents.

The Synergy, developed by Digital Keyboards Inc. of New York, is a real performers' instrument. All of the indications are that it was designed to be hauled around from the smallest gig to the largest and perhaps it is for this reason that regular storage systems like cassettes or disks were discarded in favour of a cartridge system, custom-designed for the Synergy.

The Synergy is a 48-voice digital synthesizer selling for around $5,000 -$,000. (Remember: non-American musicians cannot expect to find US originated instruments available in their home territories for a straight currency conversion price. Shipping, duty and distribution costs usually make an imported instrument more expensive in real terms.)

The 48 Synergy voices – 24 pre-set and 24 stored on cartridge – are fed to a six octave *dynamic* keyboard. A pair of sensitivity controls – one for amplitude and one for timbre – enable each player to match the characteristics of the keyboard to playing style and to the nature of the voice selected.

Four different voices may be played from the keyboard at the same time and the assignment of voices to parts of the keyboard is under

CPU (Central Processor Unit) control.

The cartridge developed for the Synergy is a passive device – it will load the programs contained on it, but it may not be used for storing anything created by the player. The cartridge looks rather like a cartridge that might be used in a TV game.

Each cartridge holds 24 new sounds and these may be loaded instantly: Crumar are developing a large library of sounds available (at a price) to Synergy users.

The control functions of the real-time section of the Synergy are programmable allowing the player to establish control over separate voices, store them and recall them when the voice is called during a performance.

A digital sequencer is built-in to the Synergy, which Crumar rather grandly describe as a 'four-track event recorder.' Each of the four tracks is polyphonic and various voices may be recorded on each track. Up to 1860 notes may be recorded and the format has been designed to facilitate overdubbing.

Great consideration has been given to the portamento section of the playing control. The rate can be set individually for each voice and many notes may be slid simultaneously, crossing over each other where necessary. The three forms of portamento offered are smooth slide, smooth slide without retriggering envelopes and semitone slide (better know as glissando).

Vibrato may be pre-programmed for a voice, allowing control to fall under the individual keys on the keyboard while the pedals offer the player traditional controls of sustain and sustenato.

The Synergy is a compromise between computer power and playability. It is a show stopper at music industry conventions and is one of the easiest instruments to demonstrate to great effect. Its price makes it attractive, but musicians will have to decide whether this compensates for lack of voice-creation abilities and interface opportunities.

A step up from the Synergy (in terms of power and facility) is the Prism – a monster of a digital synth, which is nevertheless designed with performance in mind and in its own way shuns computer approaches as much as the Synergy.

The Prism costs twice as much as the Synergy, but it is considerably more powerful. In concept it is a four octave keyboard digital synth designed for performance, but the manufacturers, Kinetic Sound Corporation of Illinois, have 'squashed' the creative power of the

The Prism. This giant keyboard is performance oriented, but is unique in offering bubble memory storage. This allows the machine to store sounds and sequences even when power is turned off (without battery back-up). The Prism is supplied with a mass of analog-type performance controls and the manufacturers will even position them according to the purchasers' specification.

micro into a performance-orientated package.

In the later chapter on dedicated music computers, it will be seen that creation of a sound is one of the major benefits available from the micro. Kinetic promote this aspect of the Prism and have developed a simple system for the musician to use this power which does not require his attention to a VDU or similar.

Another unusual aspect of the Prism is its bubble memory. The bubble memory is an excellent device providing perfect recall of information without electrical supply. Magnetic 'bubbles' move around a chip circuit built on a microscopic slice of synthetic garnet and their last position provides a map of the information stored. This expensive memory system gives the Prism great capacity — a hundred voices, a hundred patches and several hundred separate instruments. Kinetic do not publish equivalents of RAM or ROM but manage to extract this storage capacity without resorting to standard micro peripherals such as cassette or disks.

The musician interfaces with the Prism via a small calculator-type keyboard set in the middle of the instrument's control panel. In addition to numeric keys, the keypad also has a few alphanumeric and special purpose keys.

LED numeric displays and passive LEDs exist all over the console and above the notes themselves to indicate the sate of programming. This option was chosen by Kinetic rather than gathering all of this information and presenting it on a VDU.

The Prism is equipped with 24 voices (capable of handling 24 sounds simultaneously) and in use musicians may either select one of the preprogrammed sounds or may 'build' their own. The building operation starts with waveforms and a group of push-button controls offer control over additive harmony, plot or frequency modulation methods of sound building. As each of these is actually a two dimensional graphic representation of sound, Kinetic have taken a bold step in asking the musician to supply the graphics mentally whilst altering the parameters on the console.

In the additive waveform mode, the Prism adds or subtracts harmonics from the first to the 64th to create a basic waveshape. In the plot mode, the sound is created by the musician plotting 256 points on an imaginary waveform graph and in the frequency modulation mode the musician can combine modular and carrier waves with an FM index.

Once a basic waveshape has been established, control passes to a second area on the Prism called the instrument area. Here the waveshape is driven through a shaping function using nonlinear distortion techniques. The control headings are: wave blend, FM index, volume level, pitch depth, timbre value and channel mixing. The looping element used almost universally in music computers is controlled here building a short sound into a sustained sound. In this section a basic sound is turned into a voice that can be deployed under the keys.

The remainder of the Prism's controls may be grouped into two functions: interface controls and real-time controls.

The interface controls include the keypad already mentioned through which all communication with the player passes, a tuning section and an organization section where the voices created may be grouped into ensembles. Eight compatible sounds may be grouped together with any appropriate patch programs. Kinetic describe such a collection of voices as an instrument and an instrument can span anything from one key to eight octaves. LEDs over individual keys

111

indicate where each instrument's active area is positioned on the keyboard.

The wealth of real-time sound controls indicate how performance-oriented the Prism design is. Included in this section is a joystick, footpedals, four slide faders and two thumb wheels. The function of these controls may be programmed from the console and embedded in an instrument. (Kinetic also offer the option of locating these controls to suit individual musicians.) Other features designed to enhance performance include random number generators — which add an unexpected quality to an instrument — and low frequency oscillators.

The save area allows all sounds and control parameters to be saved in the bubble memory. Overall control of the Prism is conducted by an electronics enclosure which is supplied ready to travel in a flight case. Additional slave keyboards may be interfaced but there is no provision for the Prism to communicate with other computer systems. The Prism has been designed as the ultimate answer to the

The German-built PPG.2 is an unusual instrument. It is designed for performance situations, but, in the reverse of the Prophet philosophy, offers complete analog control over digital sound. The addition of a VDU and extra computing power turns the basic instrument into a 'dedicated' music computer.

heavyweight analog synth and offers some interesting ideas.

Yet another approach has been adopted by the German manufacturer PPG. In the PPG Wave 2.2 they have created a digital instrument which offers analog-type control over sound. The Wave 2.2 is also a building block which allows the musician to uprate the system into a package which becomes a dedicated music computer (see Chapter 9).

In its performance version, the Wave 2.2 is a simple-to-use 8-voice polyphonic keyboard synth which produces sound digitally. The sound sources (waves) are created by the PPG factory and stored in EPROM — electrically programmable readonly memories. These preset waveforms are held in waveform tables each of which has 64 different waveforms. The total number of waveforms available is nearly 2,000. These are loaded into the synth at the will of the user and then modified using controls which seem very close to the old familiar ADSR type knobs found on Moogs, etc.

The analog section includes controls for master tune, ADSR generators, LFO and VCA. Using the power of the host micro, the analog section has three modes, effectively trebling the functions of the set of controls.

Output from the Wave 2.2 is full blooded stereo and the keyboard can be split as desired by the performer. Equally the modes in which the oscillators work can be programmed. Several oscillators may be channelled to one small area of the keyboard (or one note) or they may be assigned in up to seven other modes.

The Wave 2.2 has two oscillators for each of its eight voices and this doubling-up allows all sorts of chorus and de-tuned effects to be created. Once a wave is selected and loaded the analog panel offers real-time sound-shaping opportunities. Patches are remembered by the Wave 2.2 and a small LCD display provides a graphic indication of control settings when a patch is loaded. This is a useful feature and one that is missing from other synths in which patch programs are stored.

A small calculator-type keypad, set in the middle of the control console provides the musician's interface. A polysequencer is built into the Wave 2.2 and cassette interface allows the programs and sequences to be dumped and stored. The sequencer is 8-track polyphonic and full editing may be carried out after recording. Volume, dynamics, keyboard sensitivity and almost every other parameter is under micro control and available to the user. Sound

113

creation is not offered, but this function belongs to the larger PPG Waveterm system.

It would be misleading to pretend that the Wave 2.2 is an analog unit and although analog controls modify the sound at one point in its production path, the instrument is purely digital in function and provides all of the editing and control power the micro has to offer. Despite its unique hardware, PPG consider the Wave 2.2 to be a soft instrument and make it clear that updating will be a matter of software rather than hardware replacement. At the time of writing, basic Wave 2.2 systems were available in Britain for around £2,000! For micro-assisted performance instruments there is no right format or package type, your choice must depend on your needs.

8 The Micro in Sequence

Computers excel wherever there is repetitious work to be done, and it is easy meat for them to store a sequence of commands and regurgitate it on demand. This function does not require much intelligence, it requires only logic-controlled memory.

Sequencers were the first taste of micro-power to be given to the musician — who will forget the startling debut they made on The Who's *Who's Next* album? The arpeggios which rippled through that record seemed (and were) inhuman in their speed and complexity. Although many sequencers are now digital, they have little connection with digital sound storage. They accept analog electrical signals, convert them to digital form for storage and re-deliver them, converted back to electrical signals, when requested. These analog electrical signals are the control voltages that govern analog synthesizers.

Most synthesizer manufacturers have been producing sequencers for some years, but they have yet to arrive at a mutually-agreed standard. Perhaps the most common electrical control standard is '1 volt 1=1 octave,' with a gate standard of 10 volts. If such a standard were accepted, all synthesizers would interface with all sequencers. They do not, and care must be taken in the selection of compatible equipment.

It is when the sequencer becomes intelligent that it becomes really useful.

When Roland introduced the MC-8 MicroComposer in 1977 few people understood it. Most music stores and musicians regarded it as an overpriced toy that might possibly be purchased by a few music colleges and the odd rock star with more money than sense. In fact it was a milestone: it was the first time the musician was offered computer power over music.

The MicroComposer was (and is) a digital sequencer controlled by a microprocessor. With simple sequencers, the procedure is usually to attach the sequencer to the synthesizer, play the part required and press the replay button. The sequencer returns the control voltages that govern note selection to the synthesizer and the notes sound in the order in which they were entered. In more advanced versions it is possible to effect some control over the signals once they have been stored: it may be possible to alter the tempo at which they are

Roland's MC-8 MicroComposer was the first computer-based composing tool on the musical market. It is a control system designed to drive analog synthesizers, but it also allows flexible composing and editing out of real-time. British hit-group Landscape considered it so important to their work that they featured it as a 'member' of the band for one album in 1979.

replayed, it may be possible to edit the sequence, replacing unwanted notes with new ones, it may even be possible to program control settings from the synth as well as pitch controls. Even with this flexibility, most sequencers remain relatively passive in nature.

The design philosophy behind the MicroComposer is simple: replace the musical keyboard with a calculator keypad and allow the human to write music into the computer. The computer can then store and regurgitate the control voltages for an external synth when required.

The MicroComposer was unsuccessful when it was first introduced, but Press attention and the belief that the device was only just ahead of its time, maintained the MC-8 in production.

Apart from the price, (around £4,000 in the UK in 1977), the main stumbling block for potential purchasers was that they didn't understand what was possible with the device. Moreover, they had to be able to read and write music and then learn a simple numeric language in order to write the music into the MicroComposer.

If the computer revolution achieves nothing else in music, it has ensured that a new generation of pop musicians has grown up with the ability to read music. The 1960s and 1970s stance of playing by ear is inappropriate in the 1980s and will continue to be so in the 1990s: the simple musical language must first be learned as a method of storing music. This language may then easily be translated into a second language which may be used for computer input. It is quite likely that as we become more used to computers we will adopt a computer-based language for written music and there is no future for music that cannot be written down and stored.

Roland say 'Programming the MicroComposer is as simple as adding columns of figures with a pocket calculator.' Actually, they're right, once the system is understood.

The MC-8 has an assignable memory. This may be used as the musician requires, splitting it down into as many as eight separate, independent voices. In fact in this mode the MC-8 may realistically be regarded as eight sequencers working in sync. The basic memory capacity of the MC-8 is over 1,200 notes and if this is divided by eight you don't need a pocket calculator to work out that each of the eight parts may hold 150 notes. This is fine for a short sequence and in this mode it is possible to connect the MC-8 up to eight separate synthesizers, push the play button and hear the eight 'invisible' players perform the piece you have written in perfect time. Most musicians will want more memory once they have come to terms with the operation of the system and an optional 16K memory pack increases total storage to around 5,300 notes – 662 notes per sequence, if memory capacity if divided by eight.

In practical use it is unlikely that eight parts will be used: typically a MicroComposer composition will use a couple of main parts with supplementary sections – middle eights, bridges, etc – being supplied by some of the other voices. In this mode the main parts may be fairly lengthy with subsidiary voices taking up little memory space.

The programs the musician writes into the MicroComposer may be off-loaded on to a cassette tape and re-stored for later use.

As already mentioned, access to the computer is via a calculator-type keypad set in the centre of the MC-8's panel. As the device has minimal control over the sound to be produced – this is set on the synthesizer(s) that will be driven by the MC-8 – the language for entering a sequence is delightfully easy. Whilst learning the language the musician must take his or her musical notation and, using charts supplied with the MicroComposer, enter each of four control paramenters. For pitch, each note is assigned a number: middle C is *24*, C# is *25*, D is *26*, and so on. If the first note is A above middle C he writes *33* in the first column of the chart. He must then write a time value for the note, a 32nd note is *4*, a 16th note is *8*, an 8th note is *16* and so on up to a whole note (semi-breve) which is *128*. All dotted notes are assigned values. After writing the time value on the chart the next consideration is 'gate time.' This is the only opportunity the MicroComposer offers for control over the timbre of each note and the gate time effects some control over the envelope the synthesizer will produce. A table of values is supplied and working with this the musician may select a suitable value and enter it on the third column of the chart. No opportunity for dynamic control is available in the resident program, but applying spare channels to this function works well.

This will probably seem a laborious method of entering music, but experience has shown that musicians are able to enter music extremely rapidly once they are familiar with the system (see the Hans Zimmer interview in Chapter 10). The chart used for learning, is dispensed with as the musician memorizes the simple numbers for pitch, time, envelope and dynamics. Thus the experienced user will be able to sight-read musical notation and automatically key the values into the MicroComposer. As may be seen from the Zimmer interview, a typical 32-bar piece of music may be entered in a couple of minutes.

The main reason for the MC-8's existence, however, is composition, and for this reason the device has a very powerful editing mode. After entering a sequence of notes with the other values for time, dynamics and voice, the musician may press 'play' and hear the attached synthesizer play the part that has been entered. During the composition process, the user will undoubtedly want to change a note, insert or delete a section or alter the timing or attack of individual notes. The piece may be stepped through: that is, the musician may press the 'step' button and listen to the music one note at a time, making deletions or insertions as he goes. Alternatively, an address location read out provides information about the location of a note or sequence in a part and the musician may go directly to this, hear it and then edit at will.

The MicroComposer is a powerful tool for the composer who is not a musician. It is an enlightening and stimulating exercise to enter a short piece of music into the MC-8. It becomes apparent that non-players have been given the facility to play if they are prepared to learn musical notation and the simple programming language.

The channels in the MC-8 may be used in ways other than those described above. With adapted programming techniques, the channels can be used to store control information over VCF and VCAs. This, of course, opens up the possibility of programming voice changes and dynamics in synchronization, with the pitch and time controls programmed into the main music parts. Some users are also

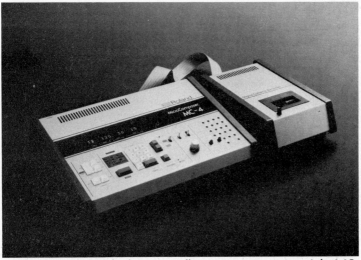

The MC-4 from Roland was a smaller, easier-to-use, version of the MC-8. Although not as powerful, this microprocessor-controlled sequencer is easy to program. It is pictured here with Roland's own high-speed digital cassette storage system.

persuading the MC-8 to store control voltages which will govern controls such as pan pots and lighting. As a result, the MC-8 is capable of offering a completely programmed sequence, provided that interface rules are observed. Other features contained in the MicroComposer include a timer display and a cycle function which allows the MC-8 to repeat stored sequences endlessly.

It took about three years for the MC-8 to become a widely-used tool in music. While this was happening, Roland Japan were working on a new model of the MicroComposer which would be easier to program and which would be less expensive. Called the MC-4, the new MicroComposer did not replace the MC-8 but supplemented it. As might be imagined, the MC-4 has the capacity to control only four independent voices, but it has several improvements in user friendliness.

With the MC-4 the inputting method has changed although the language remains the same. Pitch values for the entire sequence are entered first, then all of the time values and so on – this makes for greater concentration and more rapid input. Each note may be heard as it is entered and it is possible to enter information into the MC-4 by playing the synth to which it is connected as per conventional sequencers. Memory capacity has been increased and the standard MC-4 offers a 16K memory storing up to 3,750 notes with a 32K option pack producing a total of 48K with a capacity of 11,500 notes. Dynamic control is available on the MC-4 and this is 'CV2' (control voltage 2). This controls the dynamics (loudness) of the note and the musician may choose from a range of values between 30=ppp (very soft) and 100=fff (very loud).

An additional feature on the MC-4 is MPX output which is a relatively crude device capable of switching on and off effects such as vibrato and portamento. Usefully, each of the four channels has two independent CV (control voltage) outputs. These may be assigned to control pitch and level *or* tone.

Editing has been made easier on the MC-4 with facilities such as transposition making fuller use of the microprocessor's abilities. Default values are set by the resident software and it is this feature which really saves programming time. On 'power up' the computer assumes values such as tempo, note-time value, etc. An experienced user may change these default settings at the beginning of a long program or for more permanent use. Like the MC-8, all programs may be dumped on to cassette and Roland have now produced their own high-speed digital cassette drive system which reduces the time required for saving and loading.

The French MDP Polysequencer is a Gallic equivalent of the MicroComposer. Also offering eight independent voices, the Polysequencer offers a basic RAM equivalent to 1,300 notes spread across the eight channels which is expandable up to 5,300 notes. Parameters under control include pitch, gate and time, and full editing is provided — including transposition across 10 octaves.

Having decided against the option of trying to persuade musicians to learn a programming language, Oberheim, the innovative synthesizer manufacturer, has produced a sophisticated keyboard sequencer which takes its input exclusively from synthesizers.

The Oberheim DSX will record (store) up to 3,000 notes polyphonically — a capacity which can be expanded to 6,000 notes. The unit offers eight independently controllable CV and gate outputs capable of triggering synthesizers working on various standards. The usual features such as cassette interface and step working are provided, but the main feature of the DSX is its ease of use. It is very much like using the Oberheim DMX drum computer, and editing is simply a

The DSX is a sequencer that belongs to the Oberheim family of products. It allows full sequence editing and provides a visual display of current information.

matter of stopping the playback at the appropriate point and playing the correct note.

Until very recently, sequencers had been built almost exclusively for keyboard players. A Paris company has now built a guitar sequencer called Guitar Memory and Roland have launched a product for bass players called the Bass Line TB-303.

To be accurate, the TB-303 is both a sequencer and a bass machine, as the unit not only stores sequences but also produces analog versions of bass guitar sound. No provision is made for input from a conventional bass guitar.

The key to the TB-303 is its ability to repeat and to modify memory patterns and the success of the design hinges around the fact that bass parts are usually repetitive.

In using the device, the player keys in one bar of bass notes. A musical-type keyboard offers the user a chance to play the desired pattern rather than adopt a secondary language for programming. Although only 13 'keys' are fitted, a transpose switch converts the

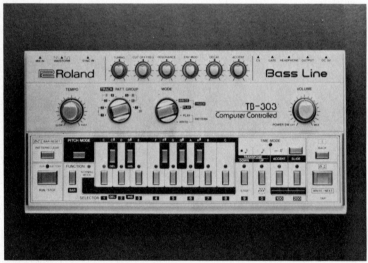

Although most computer-instruments are able to produce bass tones, the Roland TB-303 is the world's only analog sequencer especially designed for bass players who wish to build bass sequences. As with other Roland sequencers, measures are created and linked together to form complete sequences.

keyboard to cover four octaves. After entering the notes to be played in the first measure, the player then enters the time value for each note: a 16th note being the smallest available. Although the user is stuck with the bass voice built into the unit, it can be modified by accent, filter cut-off, resonance, decay and similar analog controls. A second measure of bass notes may now be keyed in using the same method and so on. These measures are stored in the unit's memory and recalled in any sequence required. Powerful editing functions make the maximum use of the small amount of available memory: e.g. a written measure may be transposed up a perfect fourth (or any other interval) by pre-selecting this requirement during the assembly of the order in which the measures are to be replayed. The measure itself never has to be re-written. In this way, the bassist may program the various parts required during a song, assemble them as required — four bars of measure 1, two of measure 2, four more of measure 1, eight of measure 2, transposed a perfect fifth, and so on — and replay them.

Sequencers may not survive as an independent unit for very long. Their function is relatively simple and most computer-based music packages offer some form of event recorder in the software. As such packages become more common, the brief reign of the sequencer may come to an end, but stage requirements will still demand small special-purpose sequencers.

9 The Mighty Micro: Dedicated Music Computers

A dedicated computer is a computer which has been built to perform one specific task. In recent years dedicated machines have become less fashionable in the commercial world: the dedicated word processor declining in favour of a multi-purpose computer. In music, however, the portents are good for the long-term health of the dedicated instrument.

Music is a discipline unlike all others. Principally it concerns the creation of pleasing sounds. Although, as we have seen, sound may easily be translated and stored in digital form, some major adaption to standard microcomputer circuitry is necessary to gain the maximum potential offered by the microprocessor to music.

In the 1960s, electronic-music students at the world's major universities waited days and weeks to gain access to large main-frame computers. When this was accomplished — often at three a.m. — their access time was limited to a few hours. In this period they had to input all of the data manually (probably a string of letters and numbers for each note of prepared music) and connect any peripheral device such as a DAC. Despite the restrictions on computing time, some of these experiments produced stunning music. But it was not a situation that encouraged musical creativity.

But in the 1970s the computer leapt off the laboratory shelf and invaded our lives and it was a natural progression for someone to develop the flexible musical package for the micro, just as it was natural for the big manufacturers to incorporate the product and use it for musical gimmicks and applications far beneath its basic power. Musical applications will never be profitable enough for microchips to be developed specifically for the art (the exception is Casio's VLSI mentioned in Chapter 4). This means that subtle and sophisticated software must be developed to adapt the capabilities of standard micros for musical storage.

Software is the most important element in any computer — dedicated or otherwise. It is software which interfaces the human with the 1s and 0s of silicon particles in the chip. There are several nests of programs in any software which is at all user friendly. The 1s and 0s in the chip itself are the basic binary language of all chips and any specialities in this are advised by the chip manufacturer. This language is embedded in the chip itself and it interfaces with the outside world via the rows of gold-plated contacts extending from the chip. (As an aside, many chips now require so little electrical current that the human touch on the inputs can overload and burn out the circuits.) It is possible to program a computer by writing all commands in the circuit's own machine language but this is slow and very time-consuming, although finally the most flexible and comprehensive method. To speed up program writing, manufacturers develop an assembly language program for their chips which allows programs to be written in a separate language that is only executed on command. This has other advantages; when writing in machine code the programmer is constantly entering and re-entering the micro memory and altering its contents. In assembly language the program will not disturb the memory during writing and will not be executed until the program is run. This allows the program to be fully developed and refined before execution. Additionally, the assembly language uses much shorthand for the long binary codes and this speeds up programming.

Above the level of assembly language there is often a user language – certainly in all dedicated music computers. This is a language that almost everybody can learn and which allows musicians access to micro power. A short instruction, written and executed in the user language, is interpreted by the more complex assembly language into the machine code that controls the micro. In addition to these three layers there have to be separate software programs written to organize ROM storage (a disk organization program for example) and software programs written for interfacing peripherals such as keyboards (both alphanumeric and music), software for ADC and DAC units and any other peripherals existing. As may be imagined, computer development relies not upon ever-increasing hardware abilities, which seems to present little problem, but upon software. The industry now talks of the 'software gap' that has opened up between hardware capabilities and man's ability to interface with the intelligence he has created.

One bright point on the horizon is that computers themselves have now been applied to the task. By using programs which write programs, the programmer is left to deal with the most important part of programming; the logic flow. In any given operation there is a logical flow of events and each of these must be tightly specified to the computer. This is the real skill in programming and a programmer may sit before a sheet of paper drawing a flow-chart of computer operations for a long period before actually writing the program. It is a profoundly intellectual exercise, most of it carried out away from the computer itself: it is an exercise in logic, in disassembling our complex world into its smallest parts and reassembling it into a language that can reach into the 1s and 0s of the micro brain.

How well software works for a particular purpose usually decides how we judge a dedicated computer's ability. In reality we are judging the software — and the package outside of the CPU. It has been found that one of the most effective ways of making software user friendly is to make it menu-driven. This phrase is a description of a software operation system which constantly presents the user with a group of options to choose from: for example, on start-up, the first display that appears may enquire whether the user wishes to create a new piece of music, edit an existing one, use the computer to sample and store external sounds, or use it for another purpose. On selection of one purpose — e.g. edit — another menu appears which asks the user the name of the piece of stored music that is required. When this is entered the computer will search the disks available to it and if the file is found, the previously recorded music will be loaded into RAM and the software will automatically set-up the screen ready for the user to continue editing or altering at any point the user chooses.

Software which is not menu driven is rapidly disappearing from consumer applications. If it were not, the user would have to learn more about programming and would have to have a basic understanding of the computer's surface language in order to call up the sub-programs that load the piece required.

Perhaps it is not surprising that the first microcomputer package dedicated solely to music production did not appear until 1980. It was in Sydney, Australia, and was named 'The Fairlight' — after a hydrofoil that skims its way across Sydney harbour.

There are about ten systems manufactured in the world which might reasonably be described as dedicated music computers. In choosing to describe the Fairlight at length I have not presupposed that it is the best, or most flexible system available. But it has now been used by a wide variety of musicians in many different countries for over two years and, as a result, considerable user feedback is available. Towards the end of this chapter, some of the other interesting music-computer systems are mentioned.

The Fairlight was the end product of five years of research by Peter Vogel, Kim Ryrie and Tony Furse. Vogel and Ryrie were, and still are, precocious young Australian designers with a talent for electronics and love of music. Furse was a computer engineer of 20 years standing who, in 1974, brought to the partnership a monster machine already capable of producing digital music. The team then developed a system called the QASAR M8 which was an eight channel polyphonic system. The unusual element in this machine was the 'dual processing' carried out by two microprocessors working in tandem. Whilst one controlled information exchange with the human users, the other saw to it that the hardware did what was necessary. The QASAR was a large expensive system and as improved microchips became available, the team redesigned the package making it both smaller and cheaper.

The Fairlight is a digital ear on the world of sound. It is markedly different to most other musical instruments in that it is capable of

The Fairlight CMI: perhaps the most advanced, certainly the most influential, dedicated computer musical instrument. This model belongs to Stevie Wonder and it is pictured here set up for one of his USA concerts.

'listening' to the external world, storing what it hears and reproducing that sound as music. The symphony of windows breaking is a reality with the Fairlight.

This ability was developed from Tony Furse's original system of digital music production. Rather than opting for FM index synthesis, or any of the other methods of sound production, he worked with digitally produced waveforms, a system that later allowed information to be entered from the outside world.

The Fairlight is larger (in total RAM terms) than most microcomputers. Its total RAM of 208k — coupled with dual processing capacity — almost brings it up to the minicomputer, the next level of computer power, although processor RAM is currently the regular 64K. The concept, successfully developed in the QASAR, of running two microprocessors as independent but linked central processing units, became a central part of the Fairlight design. There have long been problems in running separate, linked microprocessors and gaining maximum speed from both — one tends to take on capacity work leaving the other partly idle, but the QASAR development provided the answer.

As I remarked earlier, software may reliably be regarded as the really clever part of dedicated computer design. The Fairlight system contains the end product of six years of solid work by several programmers. The present program, in assembler language, occupies over 300k of memory space and understandably the team are now looking to move towards a high level language, such as 'C,' now that major improvements in hardware memory capacity are on the horizon.

Despite this insistence on the importance of good software, it is fair to say that the Fairlight incorporates some very dedicated hardware indeed. The system arrives with one or two musical keyboards (at the purchaser's option) the VDU housing the central CPUs and the eight voice modules, a dual disk drive and the main operating software language stored on an 8 in.disk. The VDU is fitted with another Furse development, a 'light pen' to assist in graphics work. The monitor was built to the Fairlight company's own design as commercially available units didn't have sufficiently high resolution to display the graphics the team wanted to use to express musical sounds and waveshapes. Some of the electronic components in the circuit have been deliberately overrated in an attempt to offer the user some protection against mains fluctuation — a phenomenon that has been known to occur on concert stages from time to time. The twin floppy disk storage system operates on DMA (direct memory access), a refined, high-speed information retrieval system. Disk systems found with most home computers and many professional machines, operate under the control of the CPU (central processing unit) which requires an interruption in the task in hand for the CPU to monitor the disk system during loading. The DMA system requires a signal from the CPU when information is required but after that the transfer takes place without the CPU being involved. The CPU senses the end of the information load. In practical terms this allows the musician to program a piece of music which calls for voices to vary during the performance, and the CPU will cue the disk to load the required voices when necessary without being interrupted in its task of controlling pitch, waveshape or any of the other parameters.

The disk drives are unimportant to the theoretical system design, but are vital in practice. Despite the expense of a Fairlight system and its relative bulk and complexity, the makers are certain that the Fairlight will become a fully-fledged truckable instrument. Several world tours have been undertaken with the system being shipped from concert to concert — in most cases without any provision for backup spares or systems being made — and the system has performed without trouble.

Fairlight financed their seemingly insane decision to build a dedicated music computer by producing business computers that Remington Office Machines of Australia shipped out as business machines under their own brand label. The hostile business environment showed up the weaknesses of available disk drive systems and the company heaved a sigh of relief when, shortly before the first Fairlight was produced, a Japanese company produced a drive significantly more reliable than anything previously available.

A Fairlight (along with some of the other dedicated instruments mentioned later in this chapter) represents the most flexible and powerful type of musical instrument available to mankind. But it has no sound of its own. When it arrives the memory spaces are empty and at no stage will a characteristic 'Fairlight sound' develop.

Fairlight Instruments provide a starting disk on which a wide variety of digitally-stored sounds are pre-recorded. These may be loaded into the Fairlight by inserting the disk into the right-hand disk drive and issuing the appropriate command via the alphanumeric keyboard

– the left-hand drive contains the system disk. The voices may also be loaded into RAM via the calculator-type keypad on the musical keyboard and via the light pen and screen. After loading, any one of the sounds is instantly available under the musical keyboard and can be played in real-time: i.e. the response time of the Fairlight CMI is rapid enough to allow instant recall of sound when a key is depressed. The operating software of the Fairlight is menu-driven throughout. On powering up and loading the system disk containing the operating software, and a disk containing sounds, an index appears on the screen. This index lists a total of 12 pages (menus) that the user may go to (several new pages are due to be added). Page 1 is the index itself, Page 2 is Disk Control, a menu for the store of voices and for the disk-control system which will create space for a new voice or file, Page 3 is Keyboard Control and this menu allows the playing parameters to be set – tuning, scale, etc – Page 4 is Harmonic Envelopes which will allow the user to draw envelopes on the screen and hear the result, and so on.

While using any of the pages except Page C ('Composition,' which loads the MCL language described later) the user may request 'Help.' This command clears the screen temporarily and lists operating instructions which should solve the user's problem. The page currently in hand is restored when the help page is no longer needed. The musician selects the page required – perhaps Page 2 to load a voice or an 'instrument' (an instrument is a generic name for a set of keyboard controls). The musician may then start to work with these. Page 2 is also the page that allows the storage of new voices or instruments to take place and the transfer of information, e.g. from one disk to another. It is the disk control page.

At any time during the user's work on a voice, a sequence or during the creation of a sound, the user may pull up any of the pages necessary and issue the next command without the risk of losing any work completed.

Most users I have spoken with say that although the system seems daunting when first delivered, basic understanding arrives after two days of experimentation and fluency develops after a few weeks. All complain that the operating manual is inadequate and poorly written, although like all aspects of the Fairlight, this is (and will remain) under revision.

The concept of the Fairlight is that, as a soft instrument the owner will never have to replace the system – the company has promised that they will never produce a Mark II which makes the Mark I obsolete. Improvements in software will be supplied on disk and improvements in hardware will be supplied as plug-in cards for the user to fit. Kim Ryrie, Fairlight's Managing Director, estimates that the cost to the Fairlight owner of keeping it up to date is a 'one thousand dollars a year.'

The keyboard unit is itself intelligent in the Fairlight package. A microprocessor is installed in the keyboard unit and this pre-processes key-strokes and control information. External controls such as pedals may be plugged into this unit and in a performance situation the VDU can be replaced by a 16 button control panel and small alphanumeric display which interfaces with the keyboard. The input commands are simplified using these buttons and long strings of pre-programmed sounds can be accessed in a shorthand form through this separate keypad. This adapts the unwieldy Fairlight package to a format as close to performance requirements as is possible.

Performance is an area that the Fairlight engineers are currently studying. Plans are afoot to provide the instrument with several new performance aids. Amongst these will be dynamic pitch-bend controls and other analog-type controls. Bob Moog — the father of modern analog synthesis — is working on a new keyboard for the company which will be pressure sensitive and super sensitive across many other areas. It will be an expensive optional extra. It is also possible that the Fairlight will become the first dedicated music computer to offer input from a guitar-type instrument. At the time of writing, a London company working in association with Fairlight, was developing a guitar-type instrument that could replace the musical keyboard. This type of input device would open up the world of the real-time music computer to the millions of guitarists who can't play a note on a keyboard.

The Fairlight CMI is an expensive musical tool. The price at the time of publication was hovering around £18,000 in Britain, plus or minus £3,000 depending on options purchased. This market position is unlikely to change. As micro-power becomes cheaper, Fairlight will opt to make the package even cleverer, rather than reduce the price of the existing system.

The eight voice modules installed in a standard Fairlight allow eight-voice polyphony or simultaneous playing of up to eight sounds. Sound can be inserted into the Fairlight's memory banks in one of several ways. The pre-recorded sounds may be loaded from disk. Most users with whom I have discussed the subject agree that the pre-set sounds are useful at the beginning, but are rapidly replaced by sounds created by the user. The second method of creating a sound for the Fairlight is to sample an external sound: the Fairlight has an input line which will accept signals from a microphone, mixer or any other line carrying sound signals. Inside the hardware an ADC converts the sound into digital form which is stored for later use.

The ADC in the Fairlight samples sound waves at a rate determined by the user (a fuller description of sampling rate is given in Chapter 3) up to a maximum of 32K. In practice the optimum rate will depend on the nature of the sound to be recorded. The duration of sample that the Fairlight is capable of taking is one area where the system has been surpassed by its rivals (although any disadvantage in this fast-moving field is likely to be temporary.) The duration depends on the frequency of the sound to be sampled. A bass drum may be sampled for about four seconds, whereas a high harmonic spectrum sound will be sampled for about one second. To overcome the shortage of sample, the waveform is looped so that it may be sustained indefinitely. Some of the shortfalls of this sampling system may be overcome by setting internal high and low-pass filters to narrow the frequency bandwidth the computer has to sample. The limitation with this system is that some fidelity of reproduction is lost – particularly at high frequencies. (The reason for this is logical: the higher the frequency, the more rapid the soundwave and the more information there is to be measured.)

Two revisions are now in hand in the Fairlight camp to redress this situation. In the short-term the company has produced a new software program which is improving the looping system, allowing users to loop a sustained sound more easily. In the slightly longer term – towards the end of 1983 – the company is uprating the hardware in the system and offering an increased sampling rate and duration, as the cost of memory chips continue to fall.

To sample an external sound, a microphone or line input is connected to the inputs marked mike or line, and Page 8 'sampling' is selected. On this page the user specifies the sampling rate to be used (examples are given in the operating manual), sets the parameters on which the high and low-pass filters will work, and provides setting for trigger level (this determines how loud the input must be before the sampling process starts) and trigger delay levels.

When the sound starts, the computer samples the sound and displays

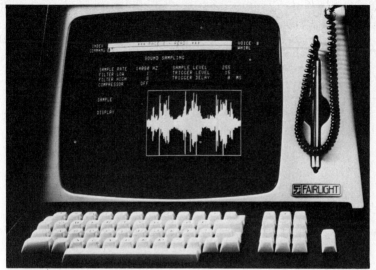

The 'shape' of a sound, as displayed on a Fairlight screen. This sound has been 'sampled' from the natural world by the Fairlight and displays the dynamic peaks and troughs that make up the sound.

a graphic representation of the waveform amplitude envelope on the screen. If the sound is required to be used in sustained form, decisions about looping must be made at this stage, and after the voice has been sampled satisfactorily, the user may recall Page 2, 'File Control,' and order the voice saved.

If a middle C from a Steinway grand piano is captured using a high-quality microphone and the note is sampled by the Fairlight, the sound may be stored on a disk as a voice. The voice may be recalled (from Page 2), stored in the 16K RAM voice modules and reproduced at will by the user. In raw terms the user may choose the sound to be reproduced at middle C and the 'piano' sound that is reproduced is virtually indistinguishable from the original acoustic instrument. Any alteration to the sound will come from loudspeakers and their enclosures, but remember that if recording is the goal, the acoustic will suffer equally when a recording of it is replayed through loudspeakers.

Without any further modification the user may then play the grand

133

piano sound back at any pitch, using the musical keyboard. In raw terms, the digits representing the timbre and envelope of the middle C remain unchanged, but the digits governing frequency are those of upper C. Thus a sound like a top C is produced but it doesn't sound like a grand piano. The reason is that the envelope and amplitude of the top C on the piano changes as well as the frequency, but the digital store did not have this information.

One answer available at the time of writing is to take several samples from the grand piano keyboard, from top to bottom. The Fairlight has eight voices, each may receive a sample from the grand piano. Now the computer has a store of information from a range of sounds. This store may be organized so that the nearest appropriate sample may be used to generate the piano note required. Thus A above middle C (A=440) would draw its envelope and amplitude from the sample of C above middle C — its nearest sample source. This is far more accurate, and for some purposes will produce a sound acceptably close to the grand. But in filling up all eight voices with separate samples, the polyphony has been used up and thus the object is defeated.

A better option would be to take the eight samples and then ask the computer to work out what percentage of which sample should be applied to the note called for. Software changes are now becoming available which will compute these changes but the reduction in polyphony still remains directly proportionate to the number of samples taken.

I have deliberately picked the piano as an example as it is one of the few instrument sounds that the Fairlight, and its rivals, find impossible to reproduce accurately. It is important to say that no musician would use a computer to reproduce a piano, it would be far better to use the original instrument. In a survey of users, Fairlight discovered that the single most important feature on the instrument was its ability to capture natural sounds and place them on the music keyboard and the computer's ability to reproduce conventional instrument sounds was rated as a low priority.

However, the problem of inaccurate reproduction should be solved when the promised new hardware is available for the Fairlight. This is scheduled to appear towards the end of 1983. Although this new hardware will retrofit all Fairlights, it is quite a major revision. The central 6800 CPU is to be replaced with the new (but related) 6809 which works internally as a 16-bit processor and offers a RAM of

256K as opposed to the existing 64K. This major jump – accompanied by similar upward leaps in individual voice card RAM capacity – will end most of the limitations now affecting the Fairlight. Sampling rate will go up to around 40K and this will make possible every kind of natural sound sampling. Currently the Fairlight has difficulty sampling long sounds, such as running water, because of limited RAM storage in voice channels. With the new capacity, quite long sounds – six seconds for example – may be captured. The bandwidth will jump from its present low-ceiling cut-off to the point where almost perfect fidelity will be possible. With this combination of new hardware and software the eight voices from the grand piano discussed in our hypothetical example will be stored in just one of the eight voices available. Accurate sound and full polyphony will be the result.

Like the more modest Prophet synthesizer (Chapter 6), the Fairlight software offers the user absolute control over the musical scale in use – this is accessed from Page 3, Keyboard Control. The default setting the software specifies is the equal-tempered scale, but a few key strokes alter this scale at the user's will. The grand piano can become perfectly tuned for the first time in its life.

It must be pointed out that although the perfect reproduction of a grand piano or any conventional instrument is a highly useful tool, particularly for recording and composing, to use the Fairlight exclusively for this purpose would be to miss a major advantage.

All sound produced by conventional musical instruments is artificial. The only reasonable definition of musical sound is sound which is pleasing and the Fairlight, and some others in its class, allows the composer and artist to use sounds from our environment in a musical way. Thus a sample of a chain saw, a canary's song or an explosion, may be sampled at its naturally-occurring frequency and stored digitally, allowing the mighty-micro control of all its elements.

Using sounds from outside the conventional sources of music has already produced a wealth of interesting and successful music – see Chapter 10 for artists' views – and as the public ear is weaned away from expecting traditional sounds to form the basis of music, so natural sound itself becomes a palette for the musical artist. This freedom has already led to some bizarre musical experiments, but market forces will finally ensure that what is most pleasing will be most successful.

Much of the music that is now produced with computer aid still apes conventional instruments, but this is changing. The composer is required to shake free from mental prejudice about musical sounds and start experimenting with sound itself all over again.

Experimentation with the essence of sound is at the centre of the philosophy that is behind the design of the third system for entering sound into the Fairlight's memory banks. This system allows the user to create sound by a variety of abstract methods. The best known of these is additive harmonic synthesis which is based on Fourier transforms, which are a series of formulas creating a bridge between the dimensionally complex relationships of frequency and time. The human ear hears sound and the mind notes the frequency, but when stored, the time elapsed must also be recorded and stored. The Fourier mathematical principle shows that all repeating waveforms can be resolved into sine-wave components, consisting of a fundamental and a series of harmonics at multiples of the frequency.

In use, additive synthesis allows sounds to be built up one harmonic layer at a time. Arbitrary waveform synthesis is also possible,

Bob Moog, the 'father' of analog synthesis, is now designing a 'super sensitive' keyboard to interface with the Fairlight. He is seen here working with the 'light pen' on the Fairlight screen.

demanding the maximum from the user and a system, unique to Fairlight, allows sounds to be drawn on the screen with a light pen. This last method of creating abstract synthesis is particularly intriguing. The light pen may be used to draw harmonic envelopes or actual waveforms on the VDU – from Page 4, Harmonic Envelopes. The light pen is also able to adjust index information on the screen and a total of 128 waveforms may be created and loaded in the waveform memory of each voice module.

When shaping harmonic envelopes with the light pen, up to eight may be shown at a time, the fundamental harmonic being shown in bold, although recent software revisions allow the 'energy' and 'duration' profiles to be displayed bringing the total envelopes that may be shown on the screen at one time up to 34. The desired harmonic number is selected by the light pen and the pen may then be used to modify an existing envelope or draw a new one.

The light pen may also be used to insert notes on to a traditional staff for composition, but an interesting comment appears in Fairlight's original instruction manual for the MCL composition language. Here the manual's author states that techniques such as the light pen are not as useful (as more orthodox methods) for composition: they are visually appealing but not as practical as inputting from musical and alphanumeric keyboards (this was written before new software improvements.)

An alternative method of abstractly creating sound is offered from Page 5, Waveform Generation. Here the musician is presented with a graphic representation of 32 'faders' such as might be found on a mixing desk. These faders each represent a harmonic in a sound. A light point on each represents the level of volume in each harmonic. This level may be altered by the light pen or by using the alphanumeric keyboard. A voice must be either loaded from disk or newly created before this page can operate. On start up this page displays the appropriate amplitude plot of the voice held in RAM. This voice may be modified as described and then saved.

Page 6, Waveform Drawing, allows sound to be created by drawing waveforms. As might be expected, sounds are saved via the control page, Page 2. With this facility, waveforms are put directly into waveform memory by drawing waveshapes on the screen. A plot function ensures the light pen is followed no matter how complex the route and 'Join' allows the user to input dots at various stages on the wave and the Fairlight computes the gaps and joins them up. The main advantage this method has over methods such as additive synthesis is that the harmonics involved are automatically computed as the wave shape changes. Joining up separate wave shapes is also made easy, with the Fairlight guessing the correct bridging shapes under the merge function.

Page 7, the control page, is loaded when ever a voice is loaded into RAM. This page allows the musician to specify the limits of such events as sustain, level, filters, attack, vibrato depth, etc: the sort of controls found for voice-shaping on an analog synth. A new software modification will marry this page into individual voice files.

Sound sampling is controlled from Page 8 and the sequencer section of the Fairlight is accessed from Page 9, Sequencer. The sequencer is programmed by playing the music keyboard in real-time. Key velocity information, foot pedal movements, etc are automatically recorded. Sequence lengths are limited by the space available on the disk: an empty disk will store about 50,000 notes. Disks are the subject of much research in Sydney. Hard disk, an advanced version of the floppy disk, allows huge amounts of information to be stored and retrieved rapidly — typically two or three million bytes against 500,000 on a standard 8 in. floppy — but the systems are too fragile for road use and Fairlight's declared policy of making the Fairlight performance proof currently excludes their great storage power. The company is offering a 'use-at-home' hard disk option whilst they research how to toughen-up hard-disk systems. (The Canadian McClevyier dedicated instrument also claims to be a performance instrument whilst offering hard-disk storage.)

Up to eight separate parts may be overdubbed — each having its own voice. Page 9 requires control decisions such as a name for the sequence and speed for playback. A sequence is recorded by using the light-pen to select record. The part is then played. To hear the sequence played back, the musician uses the light pen to select 'replay.' The speed of replay must also be selected. Parts using the same voice may be merged and all settings may be stored on disk along with the sequence.

Future software revision will allow Page 9 to write as a high level language controlling the MCL composition language described later. Page L is the Disk Library. This allows the updating of a list of files; voices, control, instrument files, etc. Whenever a new voice or other file is saved it can be added to the library list.

Page C loads the Music Composition Language that Fairlight have developed to aid composers and provide musicians who cannot play keyboards with a way to play their compositions on the Fairlight. It is also true that someone who cannot play *any* musical instrument but who understands the theory of music can compose and play with this system. This software opens up the world of music to those with imagination and a little theoretical knowledge but who have not mastered the discipline of a musical instrument – singers for example. This is likely to prove a very exciting development. The Fairlight survey also revealed that 70% of uses who *can* play a keyboard still choose the use MCL for some purposes.

The language also allows the creation of music that would be impossible to play on a conventional instrument: perhaps because the part is too complex for even the most skilled player or perhaps because the sounds used do not emanate from a conventional musical instrument. For example, the Fairlight can make minute timing decisions – down to about one millisecond – which allows very subtle rests to be written. This can be used to offset the danger of mechanical accuracy making a piece sound lifeless, but may also be used for musical effect or sounds effects such as flanging. It should go without saying that conventional composition is aided by the significant labour-saving possible when using a Fairlight with MCL – although initially, programming seems a little tedious.

Like the Fairlight's operating software, the MCL software is menu-driven throughout and a great time-saving is achieved by the constant default values the software offers. This allows the musician to accept default values (for note time value, bar length, etc) wherever possible and eliminates the need for endless input of repetitive information.

Fairlight describe MCL as being a tree-structured language operating on several levels of hierarchy. Top of the tree is the 'Piece,' followed by the 'Part' and finally the 'Sequence.' These are all terms musicians are familiar with and throughout MCL, musical language is adopted wherever possible.

A piece consists of up to eight parts to be played simultaneously and each part consists of up to 32 sequences which are played sequentially – although a larger number of sequences may be written and the overflow stored on disk. Fairlight suggest the analogy of parts representing independent musicians, each playing their own instruments through written sequences. Each part is independent although capable of playing at the same time.

Continuing Fairlight's imagery; the piece is the conductor, instructing each part when to come in. The system has the power to allow chords inside each individual part and each part may be played by a different voice. Each sequence may be between 1 and 2,000 notes long and individual sequences may be used by individual parts independently.

To to question, 'what's the longest piece of music I can compose and have played back at one time?,' Fairlight respond, 'that depends.' The final answer is that it is adequate for most purposes. Certainly piece lengths of 30 minutes or an hour usually present no problem. In use, the composer has to write a program for his music. It is this hurdle that some manufacturers (makers of the Synthia, described elsewhere, for example) believe musicians are unwilling to make. Substantial sales of the Fairlight over the last few years indicate that some musicians are prepared to learn a simple programming language, but Fairlight also think that this requirement is a barrier to expression for some users and have just produced a software revision which adds a new option called Page R to the system. Page R is described later.

It takes a little time to learn the Music Composition Language and like any learning task in life, success depends upon motivation. As may be seen from the interviews with artists using Fairlights in the next chapter, the motivation appears to be intense when absolute control over music is the goal.

The program the composer has to write in order to score a piece of music is really a program on top of a program. It is an ordered series of instructions to the computer to carry out sequential steps. As in many computer programs, each command has to be numbered. The clever software of the Fairlight provides automatic numbering, the first line being 10, the second 20, the third 30 and so on, although the user can define his or her own own numbering method (e.g 1, 2, 3, 4) to be used. It is common computer practice to space lines of command in units of ten to allow later commands to be inserted between existing lines. In music composition the numbers have the second use of allowing a musician to find a particular point on the score if a written note is taken whilst working.

The MCL program includes a 'debugger,' a self-diagnostic device that tells the user if any errors have occurred during the writing of the program. Writing programs can be tedious and it is all too easy to mis-spell a command. The usual result is that the program execution stops, or hiccups over the command. In the MCL program, the software locates the line written incorrectly and prints it on the screen for the user to amend. A debugger is a valuable timesaving device – wading through a lengthy program trying to discover why it won't run can take forever.

In common with good computer-programming practice, the MCL language allows the user to insert remarks in the program which are intended for the user's reference and which will not interrupt the program.

To write a piece of music into the Fairlight the composer opens a 'piece file' (top of the tree) and specifies how many parts there will be: part A, part B, etc. The composer then opens one of the 'Part Files' – Part A for example – and specifies how and what the sequences will play: sequence 1 will play keyboard area number 1 and sequences 2 and 3 will play keyboard areas number 2 and 3 etc. The composer then opens the first sequence file. It is here the user starts to write musical notation. Although the sequence of events calls for a specification of numbers of parts and sequence allocation before getting down to writing the dots, these decisions may be altered endlessly during composition.

Typically a composer might always start by deciding to write four parts, each of four sequences and all sequences to play on one keyboard. That might be considered *the composer's* default setting. Only as the part progresses might the composer decide to add more parts or to change around the allocation of sequences to different voices. The composer can go back and do this at any stage.

Working with a computer means endless decision-making and the first notation decisions the Fairlight composer has to make are as follows: the Beat. This is the number of sub-divisions within each time unit. Setting a value of 16, means each beat has a subdivision of 16 available. The gap specifies the time between the end of the current note and the start of the next note and it is calculated in beat units. Octave specifies in which keyboard octave the specified note falls. Transposition adds an offset to the note requested; e.g. a note which is a specified number of keys up or down is played instead of the original note. Velocity specifies the key velocity used when playing the note and the data is used exactly as if it had come from an actual keystroke on the musical keyboard. Key selection allows the key to be set, so many sharps, flats and naturals. Most of these control options have default values and the composer will be able to settle for these on many occasions.

Once these parameters are established the entering of the notation may begin. Each note may be fully specified by pitch, velocity, time and gap. For pitch the name of the note is typed in: A, D or F for example. Any accidentals may precede it, over-riding the key signature set up in the sequence specification.

Each individual note may have its own velocity specified and each note will have its time expressed in the number of beats. The gap, between the conceptual 'key release' and the start of the next note will also be set. In practice the pitch of the note must always be set, in other instances the controls for time, velocity and gap may be default settings taken from the information entered when the sequence controls were specified. Rests may be entered by an R. Notes to be played together as chords are grouped in brackets.

In this way, and with quite a few other control specifications, music may be entered. The procedure becomes rapid with practice and several composers insist it is a very efficient way of writing music. Despite this, Fairlight have produced Page R so that musicians may compose on the Fairlight without having to learn MCL. Kim Ryrie describes this system as 'working rather like a Linn Drum machine, but with the ability to add melody and expression' and the system allows the composer to build bars which constantly repeat. The composer can play notes in real-time which are read by the Fairlight and appear as notation on the screen. Adding another few bars builds up a sequence. Instruments may then be added to that polyphonically. Each pattern created can be linked together in chains (as in a Linn) and the Fairlight user has up to 250 patterns to link together. Any eight patterns can be linked together to form up to 26 sections (labeled from A to Z.) Patterns and sections can be mixed during linking to create a complete piece. It is a step by step creation in real-time with the Fairlight correcting the player's inaccuracies. The user selects the resolution (should the user want fine inaccuracies to appear) and all information regarding touch sensitivity is encoded from the keyboard. Once the whole piece is recorded, further musical lines may be played over the top of it.

Software is being developed to make Page R and Page 9 (the real-time sequencers) act as real-time input sources for MCL. The music created through these pages in real-time will write itself as MCL in the Fairlight memory. For editing the musician can then refer to the MCL read out and edit through this language – a precise and easy-to-use system. With the new high-level language that has been created in these software up-dates, Fairlight have overcome the requirement for the musician to learn programming techniques. As microprocessor memory capacity increases, so the demands made upon the musician's non-musical abilities will shrink further.

The ultimate goal for the Fairlight team is to develop the CMI so that it is totally software based. Such a system would have an analog-to-digital converter at one end, a massive amount of RAM and some super-high-speed processors in the middle and a few digital-to-analog converters at the output end. This system will arrive within a few years. Once this happens, hardware development is effectively at an end and the software teams will then have no limit to the programs they can write.

With its ability to 'listen' to the sounds of the outside world and then place them under the musician's control, the Fairlight represents the current state of the art in commercial computer musical instruments. Other systems with similar power are now available (although they use different methods to create sounds) and some have increased memory capacity, differing design philosophies, and better options in some parts of the software. Such machines are the GDS (General Development System) from Crumar, the McClevyier (a digital/analog hybrid made in Canada) and the Synclavier 11, a second generation of an early dedicated instrument.

At the time of writing, the GDS is significantly different to other dedicated systems – perhaps with the exception of the PPG Waveterm – in that it provides extensive analog-type physical controls on its musical keyboard as a means to facilitating performance use. This reflects the philosophy behind the GDS design, which clearly considers that the musician will be unable to relate to a typewriter-style keyboard or written control information and would like to use physical means of entering control data. Much of the information, which on the Fairlight and similar systems is now entered on the alphanumeric keyboard, is entered by the physical knobs, sliders and switches arranged above the musical keyboard. An alphanumeric keyboard is supplied with the system, but in performance its use is limited to changing the assignment of the physical controls on the musical keyboard. As will be seen from the earlier descriptions of the way Fairlight sees the market, most companies are now beginning to wonder how the musician will relate to programming techniques.

An interesting problem-solving technique used on the GDS concerns the variation in timbre that occurs when an instrument is played in different ways. When a piano key is struck hard, is has a different timbre to when it is played softly. In the GDS 'Timbral Interpolation' system, the voice is assigned two timbres, one hard, one soft. The velocity-sensitive keyboard feeds information to the microprocessor about the velocity with which the key is struck and the microprocessor computes this velocity as one of 32 areas between hard and soft. The timbre of the voice is selected accordingly and drawn from one of the 32 options computable between the two basic sounds representing each end of the spectrum. Of course the sounds specified by the musician to make up each end of this spectrum may be radically different, allowing the musician to change between dramatically different sounds simply by increasing or decreasing keyboard velocity. A similar 'interpolation' program exists between parameters set for filter structures. Control of these filters is assigned to keyboard-mounted joysticks during performance and their position offers control over which of the 32 stages of filter are applied at any given time.

Many other features are included in the excellent, but also expensive, GDS system, which is a compromise dedicated system, trying to straddle the demands of both the performer and the user who wishes to utilize the great power the micro has to offer.

The problem of how to make these powerful systems user-friendly is occupying all manufacturers. Another approach has been adopted by the German maker, PPG. The PPG Wave 2.2 is described in Chapter 7, but the company has built this performance-oriented keyboard in such a way as to allow subsequent upgrading to a more powerful system. With the addition of a second microcomputer unit, a disk drive and a VDU, the system may fairly be considered dedicated.

The uprated PPG system is called the PPG Waveterm and the additions to the keyboard are housed in a single 19 inch flight case which is mounted on brackets and suspended above the keyboard. The case contains a VDU screen, ten numeric buttons and a 8 inch disk drive.

Perhaps the most surprising element in the Waveterm package is that provision has been made for sound sampling, in a manner which has some similarities to the Fairlight system. The package is not nearly as powerful as the Fairlight – it is far less expensive – but it also allows natural acoustic sounds to be entered into the system via mike or line and then used as a voice for the polyphonic keyboard. There is no alphanumeric keyboard supplied with the Waveterm and PPG insist that the system can be used by anyone, even those with no knowledge of programming. The 20 numeric keys are laid in a row immediately beneath the VDU screen and, as with most microprocessor controls, a number of the keys (ten) are assignable for various functions. To assist the user in remembering what the buttons do in what mode, a small portion of the screen above the buttons always states what function each button currently has.

Additive synthesis is also offered by the Waveterm. As in the Fairlight and several other creative computers, Fourier transforms are used to compute gaps between harmonic amplitudes, but the Waveterm, as well as offering the usual sine wave base, also allows an already formed wave to be used as a fundamental on which to build. Additional abstract-sound-creation possibilities are offered by the manipulation of wavetables.

Natural sounds entered from the mike or line input may be displayed as envelopes on the VDU. Adjustment of these envelopes is possible and a zoom facility allows a small part of the envelope – such as the beginning, or 'attack' – to be shaped with great precision.

The system is able to offer a greatly enhanced sequencer which PPG describe as an event generator. The software in this sub-program allows considerable flexibility in editing and joining sequences.

The PPG is a dedicated system that is almost completely performance oriented. My earlier remarks about the unsuitability of dedicated systems for regular gigs, apply less to this system than to others. But although the system's ability to create music out of real-time is considerable, it is limited in comparison to music-writing software such as Fairlight's MCL language and Page R. The choice of system finally rests on what you want it to do and how much money you can afford.

The dedicated music computer is still in its infancy. In ten years' time systems now available will be seen as having been expensive, clumsy and limited in power.

As microprocessor costs come down, Fairlight have expressed their intention to increase facilities rather than allow the system to slip into a cheaper price range. Dedicated systems with complete power over the creation of music and sound will never be dirt cheap, the hardware and lengthy programming necessary ensure that. But the sort of power now offered by such systems will be available in *much* cheaper systems in a few years. The manufacturers who are as dedicated to perfection as their machines are to music will concentrate on offering greater and greater power. As Kim Ryrie of Fairlight makes clear, the ultimate goal is an instrument that is completely soft. This system will demand massive RAM and processor power and an even greater level of software sophistication, but once achieved, the composer and the musician will be offered an unlimited range of sounds to turn into music and unlimited methods of writing and performing that music. Such a system is likely to be available by the end of the 1980s.

10 The Micro and the Musician

Warren Cann

'If you have a rhythmical mind, you don't *have* to learn technique, you can buy a Linn — or something like it.'
Warren Cann

Warren Cann is the percussionist and electronic guiding force in Ultravox. He was brought up in Vancouver and Los Angeles and has studied towards a degree in electronics. In the Ultravox stage act, much of the rhythm is pre-programmed.

'My first programmable instrument was one of the original Roland TR77 rhythm units. I tapped into the clock's voltage and found a very cheap and dirty way of getting my tempo read-out. Whatever the clock's at, you have it as an arbitrary figure, but it works as a reference point.
'I am very attracted to never-varying rhythm, but when you're using a programmed rhythm on stage you can't be a slave to it, you've got to push it around. You have to take into consideration human feelings: the psychology of playing with machines in real-time is a whole subject on its own.
'If everyone's a little tired they will turn around and swear blind to me that I'm playing too fast. If everyone's buzzing and there's great audience reaction, they will swear, equally sincerely, that I'm dragging. So you have to be able to accommodate such needs in a myriad of differing situations whilst using programmed rhythms.
'With a good programmable drum machine you can make very fine changes in tempo that have a tremendous effect on the feel of a song, but which you wouldn't notice normally.
'I'm very accustomed to playing to a machine tempo now, but the thing I noticed over the first few months was that my timekeeping was very sloppy. Acclimatization to playing to a machine doesn't take long, but I had always prided myself on being a good

Warren Cann at work with his Linn Drum. Warren was one of the first percussionists to not only accept programmed rhythms, but to develop a new style of playing from the challenges they present.

timekeeper, and I realized just how often everyone unconsciously makes corrections for everyone else in a band. You might be a little bit early coming out of a fill or, more often than not, late, or when you hit a chorus everybody just naturally speeds up and they don't realize it. These are not things you can discern, they are just part of the feel.

'It took me about a month to get used to machine tempo and then I started really getting off on it. I used to think: 'it's not really me against the machine.' After that initial hurdle, I applied myself towards totally overcoming any real or imagined unease regarding playing acoustic drumkit accompaniment to electronically generated rhythms.

'Sometimes, in the studio, we've placed an acoustic snare drum on the track and later we've decided to beef it up, with a Linn Drum snare. I found out that my timekeeping is now usually within one hundredth of a second or some such ridiculous amount and always slightly ahead of the beat.

'I started to love the idea of playing with machines. A lot of musicians hate playing to click tracks, it doesn't bother me. Only rarely is it unsuitable and that would be in a song that needs drags and pushes.

'I found that I really enjoyed the effect working with machines had on my time-keeping. In most of the stuff I record now, the drums go on last...or, if there are any drums which have to go down from the beginning, I keep very strict time during the number, just as a guide track. Mostly I prefer to work with a click track.

'The other musicians in the band didn't appear to notice me turning myself into a metronome! They noticed that everything felt a little bit more solid.

'It is a little less flexible working with a drum machine, but that is also totally dependent on context. If somebody misses an entry into a chorus everyone decides 'all right, once more around the park.' If I suddenly punch in the wrong beat, it's sometimes a lot more obvious, depending on the pattern for that section of music. Normally I'd be able to cover it up.

'We could gloss over fluffs quicker in the early days of drum machines than we could now because the beats changed immediately on pre-select rather than at the beginning of each bar.

'After the TR77, I got hold of the Roland CR78. I was fed up with playing the 77, I felt like a one-armed paper hanger with it. I had found out that if I held in two or more of the buttons at the same time, I could get all of those rhythms playing simultaneously at the same tempo. So I was stuck there with my fingers holding the relevant buttons in all the time. It was torture, one little slip and things would screw up. It got to be just crazy trying to get through a song, I had to bastardize an instrument far beyong the wildest dreams of its original designer to get what I wanted. The realms into which I was taking it meant I had to go all round the houses 20 times to get from one beat to another. I was constantly trying to think of ways to outsmart the machine.

'Programming is a very elementary skill. What you are doing is in essence no different at all to the thought processes necessary for playing in real-time. As a player you think the way a drum machine will think after it has been programmed. You store in your memory a range of basic beats that you like – actually there's not that many,

I'd be hard pressed to think of 20 before the variations start and excluding the Latin American rhythms. So you compile a vocabulary of drum beats and you dip into it all the time. You decide; 'all right, I shall start with this beat, then I'll change to this beat and then I'll go back to this beat. During this part of the verse I'll slip in this little variation'... and so on. You do that without thinking about it. You just transfer that process to the machine. It's like the analogy of walking over and picking up a glass of water and having to program a machine to do the same thing. You just have to analyze all the movements. You suddenly realize that all things you take for granted are part of a *program*. There is essentially no difference to working out of real-time, you organize yourself before hand, physically, because you're utilizing a physical method of expression and need to have achieved a degree of technique for its satisfactory execution. 'Drummers haven't had the same technological advantages that other musicians have had — at least not until now. All of the instrument companies, all of the R&D departments, were geared to synthesizers, not drum machines. Synthesizers actually took off even quicker than they had hoped for. Within a very short space of time they were no longer the exclusive, esoteric property of people like Keith Emerson, Mr Moog, W.Carlos or whoever. Everyone was suddenly pouring all of this development into making synths better, then it kind of levelled out. Aside from the digital/analog split, everyone then started work on human engineering. Narrowing that gap between the initiation of an idea and its conclusion is marvellous...actually giving you more physical contact with the instrument through, say, vibrato pads rather than a rotary dial or so on, is very important.

'I've been off in left field, trying to get something out of electronic percussion and its programming. Nobody was doing anything about it. I have had to spend five times the amount of time working on these machines to the point where I felt I was getting the same kind of versatility with them that I would have had they been conventional synthesizers.

'The first thing I did on getting the CR78 was to establish its shortcomings — I mean I was happy to have its advantages, but I was immediately concerned with its shortcomings and how to overcome them. They turned out to be, principally, capacity and flexibility. I started making all kind of serious modifications to it, like I had to the TR77. I used the same stunt for tempo and made little mods all round. Looking at the service manual, I found out that there was a trim pot inside to control the decay on the bass drum. That was important: The way it comes from the factory...I'm sure it sounds like a bass drum at a fairly low level, but if you put it through the magnifying glass of the studio or the sonic afterburner of 20,000 watts, it's not a thump any more it's a boooooooing! So I shortened the decay and adjusted for the curve of how the human ear responds to treble versus bass. As soon as I was dealing with that kind of volume, I had to pull the snare drum back because it was no longer in a comfortable balance with a bass drum. I'm sure no one in the Roland factory took a CR78 and put it through 20,000 watts of amplification − or even a 1,000 watts.

'I ended up spending a great deal of time and money to get it right for my application − time I would have been far happier spending with the rest of the guys writing songs rather than conferring with my engineer over circuitry. I didn't really want to get involved in that side of it, I just wanted to explain what had to be done and have it happen. My engineer didn't really know what I was trying for and I had to keep very close to him as he was working on it.

'A lot of the programming in the band has come from me, but the rest of the guys were very hot on any kind of memory capability and sequencing. The very first thing I did after getting the two drum machines was to improve the amplification set up. It is very difficult to find the right kind of amplification for drum machines. I experimented with everything − from lots of little speakers to huge bins and horns. Believe it or not, I now use a pair of Yamaha columns with 16 ten inch speakers. I get a very fast rise time from them, no unwanted colouration, and they're extremely impactful − the lows and highs from those speakers suit percussion incredibly well. It still amazes me that the speakers can handle it. I've got the grills off them and I can see them going in and out − the travel is well over an inch − I know I'm just on the threshold of blowing them up.

'My interest in programming spread to the rest of the group and the links started appearing. Chris wanted to use sequencers with the option to overdub in sync when we were recording and I didn't want to commit myself to first takes either, so I thought 'there must be a way.'

'So my engineer and I got together and we built a little box that took the clock and changed it into an audio signal which we could put on to tape and then convert back to a clock. So, a little by-product of this was that I realized that these pulses that came from the clock in my drum machine could control something else. If I had a switch which switched pulses off and on I'd have a little sequencer. I realize now that I had reinvented the MicroComposer sync code. At least mine was cheaper!

'So that was a useful development of what was originally a sync facility which we would use before doing over-dubs which would then let us go over it and add something. There was no other way of doing that at the time – the Linn was a long way away.

'Chris and I initially linked up his Moog to my sequencer and we had some very happy accidents. The control voltages would change inadvertently: I'd be changing all the gates and when I put a rhythm through he wouldn't know what was coming. I would be expecting a bass line to sound a certain way because of the way I was sending controls and he was changing the notes and he was expecting it to sound a certain way because of where the notes were occurring. We had some good things out of that.

'After a while Chris decided that even when he knew what was coming and we had things planned for songs, he wanted to control it himself. For this, I introduced two-way command links.

'We work hard toward continuity in our stage act: if there is going to be a break between numbers we want it to be there for reasons of pace, not because we need a break to program the next number, or whatever.

'We've found that we've become adept at programming changes. If you have a spare hand for five seconds you do something towards programming for the next number, or the number after that. If there is a bar's rest for me, I'll turn around and I'll make some changes. It has got to the point where on our last two tours I found that I literally had in the region of 20 to 30 total seconds spare time during a performance where I could afford to let my attention wander.

'The Linn Drum had a profound effect on me. It is a new instrument, a dedicated percussion instrument, and its arrival is truly exciting. A lot of people are now going out and buying a synthesizer as their first instrument. It is no longer something an accomplished keyboard player later buys to experiment with. People who have never played any instrument before are getting into synthesizers. Now this has happened to drummers.

'If you have a rhythmical mind, you don't have to learn a physical technique, you can buy a Linn or something like it. Now a lot of people will become very accomplished and will probably stick with being a less physical type of drummer rather than a conventional one, but their personality and their attitudes do not mean, for example, that they're not going to come up with some very John Bonhamesque things – things that just crush you against a wall.

'I had one of the very first Linn Drums in this country. It was very expensive then and it is still true that if you haven't got considerable earning power, you just can't go out and buy one of those things. Just for laughs I checked when I bought my Linn and I could have gone out and bought a new Renault 5 for what the Linn cost me. Obviously I'm pleased the new Linn is less expensive.

'To learn how to program a Linn is in some ways very, very simple and similar to programming a CR78. I just threw myself into mastering the Linn. I immediately thought 'Great, they've got this right, that right' . . . I was very excited because of all the things they had got right. After about four or five days, I suddenly started seeing all the multitude of cracks and I decided to delve into those later. I continued to exploit the machine and I feel I've really done that now, I've gone through it front to back. I probably know things about that Linn now that Roger Linn doesn't know.

'I hesitate to mention most weaknesses in the machine because I've learned how to make use of them and correct them in the studio and to some degree I kind of hate to give away a trade secret.

'I consider the Linn's contribution to be enormous; it's a turning point. I got a real buzz from it, it kept me up at night working with it....a real landmark.

'What I find peculiar is that many people regard its importance as offering real drums in a digitized form. I mean, that's great – but to me it was the programming facility that was important.

'I would like to see 100 times the amount of control that even the new Linn is likely to offer . . . after all, there aren't that many people using them live or to their full capacity on the studio.

'There have been a lot of records in the British charts recently that have got Linns on them and they've been used fairly clumsily. In most cases, you can hear the lack of imagination.

'I've been telling everybody who'll listen, something I consider important for drummers: rather than hold this attitude of being afraid of machines 'what chance do we have if we let machines come in – they can play faster and more accurately etc' drummers are the people who will get the most benefit from these things. It is not replacement of an acoustic drumkit any more than a Fairlight is going

to replace pianos. It is just new horizons. I respect people like Billy Cobham, for example, but there's no way in the world that I would want to play like him, even if I could. I don't want to spend 20 years perfecting techniques to do the things he can do because it is not exciting for me. I'm a musician before I'm a percussionist. I'd much rather play basic parts if that's what the song requires rather than every two bars try to show off a flash fill I've spent a year perfecting. 'I thought 'great' when I had the Linn. I know there's a new one, I'm due to review it for some magazines. But I'm not going to throw out my old Linn. There are some things on it that I will want to keep, some wonderful eccentricities which may be designed out in the name of progress but which allow me to do certain things. I've had the memory on it expanded to its full capacity which is very useful. 'When people have an item like a Fairlight, one would think 'Well this is it, it's the whole caboodle wrapped up in one package, all you have to do now is make that package small enough to carry in a shoulderbag.' But you are still dealing with people and there are basically two types of people; people with melodic, asymmetric minds and people with percussive, geometric minds and it is really overkill to give a Fairlight to someone who just wants to program rhythms; as well as overkill it is also lacking in many departments a drummer would consider vital. You do need something dedicated to percussion. You can write up amazing drum sounds on a Fairlight and then program them. But it just seems to me to be a bit unnecessary; drummers need very few of the other facilities a Fairlight-type computer offers. For instance, a typewriter keyboard for input is a stumbling block for many percussionists.
'The potential for teaching percussion via these things is fantastic. That's what the Linn is great for. You can be a total non-musician and in about ten minutes of reading the instructions you can be coming up with rhythms that are exciting and encouraging you. If you apply yourself you will later learn how to use them more fully, but at the same time, if you have somebody who's competent and you give them a Linn, they suddenly realize that they have to start thinking about what they've been doing. It really works.'

JOHN LEWIS

'I went through a little crisis shortly after I started to work with the Fairlight in which I started to have dreams thinking that I was a

series of numbers.'
John Lewis.

John Lewis, originally from Edmonton, Canada, is a classically trained musician and composer working mostly in London, England. He produces his own electronic music albums and supplies scores and recordings for film, television and radio.

'I first started working with electronic music in 1975. I had to write a little film score for a small documentary that didn't have sufficient budget to hire a lot of instruments. I offered to do a very simple thing if I could find a little EMS VCS3 or similar synthesizer and learn how to use it. In the end it was really just tune and bass that I played live and tried to make different sounds. I hadn't previously played any synthesizers.

'My initial reaction was one of frustration, because I couldn't get what I wanted. But I was interested. At that time I was Assistant Musical Director to the Ballet Rambert and I was writing instrumental pieces for them. I met Brian Hodgson of the BBC Radiophonic Workshop when he wrote a piece for the ballet and he offered to help me shop for some synthesizers.

'In the end I joined him in his electronic workshop venture and I came up against an EMS 256. That was the first time I moved my music-making out of real-time, my first experience with programming. I think I realized then how important a step that was, because I stopped playing as fast as possible and concentrated on the content of the pieces I was working on. Although the 256 was limited I used it right up until last year. The capacity of that instrument is 256 notes on three layers and they are really independent although they must start at the same time.

It uses a memory system called the Honeywell Shift Register, it's a live memory with no storage. But we found a way of storing stuff on tape so we had a very early digital storage system. All the information controlling a long, long stream of notes could be stored.

'We did find that we could store the time as well and when we got to our second album using the instrument we were storing control voltages on tape and playing them back from the 16-track — we could control everything, including dynamics. In the end we could store whole sequences of chords from the 256 and fire them off when we wanted to just by pressing a button.

'In the end the 256 became more and more frustrating because I

155

wanted to store more than I could, although some of the music I devised on it is very, very complex. It had to be done in little bits, putting a clock down on tape, and putting stop and start sequences down. There were two frustrations. One, we couldn't store enough music and the other was that we couldn't store the sounds. We talked about techniques of doing that, of course, but we were always thinking analog. Now we know that was a blind alley. But we thought a lot about the problem. I had the idea for huge banks of oscillators and a huge control system — it would have been prodigiously expensive. We even had a keyboard designed to go with the analog stuff. It was a 10-note polyphonic keyboard, two were made, one for me and one for the BBC. I never used mine. It works perfectly well, but one of the things was that the line-up of the oscillators wasn't sufficiently good. The drift was too much, it just wasn't satisfactory. But it was quite a good keyboard.

'Then, of course, the Prophet came along in 1977 and I rushed off to New York and bought one.

'The Prophet didn't open up all that much, actually. It was just that

John Lewis with his Fairlight. He prefers to enter musical via the Fairlight's MCL composition language rather than use the musical keyboard, despite being an accomplished keyboard player.

I could store a lot more sounds. All I used it for was overdubs. I was so into programming at this time that I wasn't interested in live-time playing.

'The first real machine I got my hands on was the Fairlight. I've had it since November '81. David Voorhouse had had his for ages, but while I knew the facility was there, I couldn't afford it. The package, including the Linn Drum I bought and financial costs, came out to nearly £25,000!

'I wasn't very computer literate when I got the Fairlight. I couldn't write Basic, for example, I didn't know about the hardware. But the discipline of programming the 256, even though it was analog, was very good training.

'I took about three weeks off to learn the Fairlight after it arrived. I just started reading the manual and going through page by page until I had done it. There are actually two manuals, one for the machine and one for the MCL language, which is the composition program.

'The MCL manual is very, very good, although with a couple of errors that need updating. The other manual hasn't been updated sufficiently — at least I don't have a copy of an updated version. A lot of the manual is now included in the 'Help' page in the Fairlight program. In a way the only hold-up in using that manual is that the concept behind the creation of sounds isn't adequately explained. But I stuck with it, I stayed on Page 4 (one of the menus in the Fairlight) trying to find out how to do it and not really getting the concept.

'About 200 programmed sounds came with the Fairlight, about ten disks with sound on them. I went through them after I had it about a month and scrapped a lot of them and renamed all the rest. The names they used didn't mean anything to me.

'I started right away creating new sounds. I went through a little crisis shortly after I started to work with the Fairlight in which I started to have dreams thinking that I was a series of numbers. I'd wake up in the middle of the night and all I could see was a number. I was spending about 16 hours a day working with it. I was determined to get to grips with this machine as fast as possible. I found I didn't write any music at all in that period. All I did was play with the machine. Then I thought 'right, I'm not going to worry about making sounds any more, I'm going to get on with programming language, MCL,' and that's when I really started to make progress. 'Once I started actually writing, then I found the answers to all the questions that had occurred. Working on it in abstract, trying to find out how the computer works wasn't very helpful. A lot of things I originally thought were ambiguous, turned out not to be.

'I think the language on the Fairlight is very straightforward, although it seems intimidating at first. I had never done any computer work, and there seemed to be so many codes, so many different control letters, but in fact I learned them in a very short time and I use them without even thinking now. Sometimes I'll make a mistake while I'm writing a program and I'll type O (for 'open') instead of E (for 'edit'), but that's just because I'm typing so fast – I'm grateful now that I learned to type properly at one point in my life. There are warnings in the system to tell you that program line so and so is wrong – the protection is there. Those warnings very seldom come up any more, I'm glad to say.

'I think working with the 256 started to narrow my composition style down in the end, I had to constantly remember what the system couldn't do and I ended up writing within those constraints. I stopped thinking about certain possibilities because I knew the machine couldn't do it. I think it closed a lot of things off. Now the computer is opening them up again. Now I expect to be able to write whatever comes into my head, I'm not thinking in limitations any more.

'In terms of sound, I'm not really interested in using the Fairlight to make it sound like other instruments. Using natural sounds for music is like having music concrete again. If you use sounds as they exist in the instrumental world and if you slow them down or whatever, they're quite interesting. It makes me think about doing pieces which are much more like old fashioned music concrete again — I mean in my own style. I don't mind using natural sounds as sources to build it and they're immediately going to hear all the clich`s. The brain is a device which assimilates selected bits of information and builds a

'Although I'm not interested in duplicating existing instruments at all or in using real sounds in my own work, I have been working a lot with clients who come in and say, 'Will you program this piece for me?' I have to do some of it, but I think it's very boring.

'I've received some vibrations about the Musicians' Union attitude to Fairlights and other computer instruments. I know other people who have Fairlights and they've had trouble. I didn't go into it myself. There's going to be a shift from the performer to the composer.

'I've been hiring out my Linn Drum because it saves a lot of studio time. It is drummers who are doing the programming, that's what is amazing me. When I did my first two albums I used live drummers on both of them and we had immense trouble. They were playing to previously recorded programmed stuff and they found it very hard. What fascinates me about drummers is that they must all now be playing to pre-programmed stuff.

'As far as performing goes, it is not that easy to perform something you have created out of real-time. What I would need would be about five Fairlights linked together. There are limitations, not limitations by conventional standards, but I've already over-stretched two areas in the Fairlight. The current memory, that which you can store from disk, is too small. They're about to update it and at least double its capacity. Because I work in such complicated pieces, I can't load all the parts and all the sequences in simultaneously any more. I can hold an eight minute piece with over 60 sequences. But that's not enough for me. All sorts of very small things require a new sequence to be created. I have worked out ways of formatting a piece — I'm working on all sorts of ways of speeding myself up. I write a part called 'The Format' which has all the spaces in it so that when I write a new part I can just plug one of my sequences into the gaps. That's been very useful.

'The other frustration, the old snag, is that it can only take eight voices at a time. I don't like to commit myself to tape until the last possible moment because I keep changing my mind. So that's why I've developed this format system. It's a great help to keep everything available so you can play against everything else. Even the disks are too small, I can't store enough sounds on them.

'Something I don't use at all is the sequencer in the Fairlight. I think I will. They're developing a new way of crossover...at the moment you can take sequences from a music programme, and use the sequence, but they're working on a method so you can go either way at any time.

'I've got so fast at programming, I don't use the music keyboard input at all. I use the alphanumeric keyboard all the time. I just sample the sound via the musical keyboard.

'Before I had the Fairlight, I used to compose at a keyboard or on paper. I have now stopped writing things down all together. I write everything straight into the Fairlight. I do sometimes cross reference when I'm doing contrapuntal things, but I don't write them in full scores any more, I just write the individual sequence and then look at it and examine it with the staves and work out the counter points.

'I'm spending a lot more time on reorganizing the pieces than I used to. I write the basic idea, maybe in a couple of hours, and then I spend three weeks working on the structure of it. I think the pieces turn out better as a result, but it is a different way of working.

'I don't know if my output has been increased, I think it has, but I'm taking a lot more trouble now. In one way, it's a lot slower. I'm taking a lot more time because I don't think I have any excuses.

'An advertising client came in: he had to have a musical logo for something, he was absolutely desperate, he had to have it almost instantly. It had to be precisely ten seconds long.

'I don't know what he expected me to come up with, but I said, 'Go away for an hour and come back.' In that time I had written the whole piece for him, I had scored it, tymps, trumpets...I was forced to use stored sounds, of course. I just grabbed a disk and used the first sound that came along. I thought 'what can I do with this sound?' He couldn't believe it when I played it. He knew it couldn't have come off the shelf . . . it was exactly to time and exactly to brief . . . he was amazed. That would have been impossible before I had the Fairlight.

'I'll tell you another great big advantage the Fairlight has for commercial work. I did a commercial for Brooke Bond tea. They came back to me six months later and they'd had a big success with the commercial and they said 'We now have to have a pack shot at the end because the tea is now in tea bags. It has to be three seconds shorter.'

'They had found out a way to speed up the video, they asked if I could speed up the music.

'I said 'Well, you know what happens, it will just sound higher.' This was last summer. That's all they were able to do, just speed it up. Well now, of course, I could edit it, change it a little, I could do it instantly...it would take five minutes.

'I have been telling people that my relationship with my Fairlight is almost adulterous. I can't over estimate the impact it has made. I'm an inherently messy person except when it comes to my music. I'm very neat about the music itself and about the detail. But now I'm even starting to catalog my tape library into this computer, even though I don't have a program for it. It thinks it's writing music, but it's my library.'

Hans Zimmer is a German, electronic musician who plays sessions in London and makes up part of Helden – an experimental band – along with Warren Cann, Ultravox's percussionist.

'We were backing a singer called Ronny at the Old Vic (London), it was her first ever live gig. She had made a record on which the entire back-track had been pre-programmed and we decided to program the music for the show. We had six days to get the whole thing together and that was an awful lot of programming to do in six days.

'The original record had been made on synthesizers, but it had been done by sticking a click track down on the multi-track tape and playing the parts at half speed. We had nothing to do with the original recordings and we had to recreate somebody else's music. Actually, I found it very hard, getting it all together on stage. We had 16 voices running at the same time. We did six numbers in 40 minutes. There was a lot to do as we tried to get the live sound as close as possible to the record.

'We used a Linn Drum for Percussion and Warren (Cann) was playing his Symmons synth-drums on top of that. He didn't use an acoustic kit. I had my big Moog which was controlled by six Roland MicroComposers. I was controlling the computers but I was also playing a Yamaha piano live. I had left spaces and I was adding parts, just for the fun of it. We did the whole thing as an experiment, to see how a programmed show worked . . . we wanted to see if it was humanly possible. Everybody says, 'Oh, but you could just have a tape on stage' – it isn't the same! There's something that seems to happen the moment you're on stage and there's an audience out there. It makes the whole thing much more exciting. We didn't set up any of the sounds before we got to the venue and we were able to listen to the room and get the sounds there: especially tailored for the night – you couldn't do that with tape.

'The tracks we had to copy for this gig were fairly straightforward. They had been done by people who didn't really know that much about synthesizers . . . I knew precisely what the player has been doing, I knew which buttons he had pressed. There were quite a few recognizable sounds. They used a Linn, but because of the way we linked the Linn and the MicroComposer it was written in a different time base so we re-wrote all the parts. We had their programs and

Hans Zimmer. An experimental musician and leader of the group 'Helden.' He undertook one of the first ever live gigs which relied entirely on pre-programmed backings (not taped) at London's Old Vic theatre in 1981. In the background is a Fairlight CMI.

we listened to them. We discovered that they had been written by people who haven't really done much programming before so they were pretty clumsily put together. It was easier for us to just scrap it and start from scratch.

'The great thing about computer technology is that you can say 'what do you think about this bit?' play it immediately and then change it.

'The concert was very rushed, but very exciting. Warren was still programming as the curtain was rising just because he had an extra idea.

'For the basic tracks we used two Roland MC-8 MicroComposers and four MC-4 MicroComposers, all running in sync. I had the first three songs entered into the MC-4s because they held more memory – we got about 20 minutes worth into the four. We didn't have to load at all during the performance. With the other two MC-8s we got another 20 minutes, but the two MC-8's were playing 16 lines.

'We were all worried about how Ronny, the singer, would feel about it: knowing there's no going back! But there wasn't really a problem. We had arranged it in such a way with her beforehand that we all knew what was happening. When you work with these machines you have to be so clear with your intentions. There's no room for fumbling about. You have to know what you want to do. If you don't know what you want to do it's not going to happen.

'I do not regret not having a formal musical training. I can play piano well enough to play what I want to play. I notice a certain lack in my keyboard technique but I have a whole studio at my disposal and I can program. Of course, I can program from the keypad without having to play the part. In Helden we have a team that includes a Steve Rance, our studio engineer, Warren and myself – Steve can work the MicroComposer just as well as I can. If I tell him to put an A in, it won't mean as much to him as it will to me, but he will understand if I say 'put a 33 in.' His side of things is interesting; he is automating his mixer through the MicroComposer – putting his pans in and so on. People are always amazed at all our different pans...they can never understand how we do it. It's so bloody easy, once you have the technology.

'I first started working with a MicroComposer when I was in a small band in Brighton. I was led into it by talking with other musicians and talking with Brian Nunney from Roland UK. I always wanted to be a good piano player and for years I knew someone was going to come up with that sequencer...I had the little VCS3, a nasty keyboard sequencer, and I knew there was a better way of doing it. Suddenly Roland brought out this MC-8 and I got a bank loan and bought it along with a Roland System 700.

'The manual for the first MicroComposer was badly written, but it didn't take me that long to learn it. I allowed myself to be booked for a recording session a week after I had the MC-8 so I just had to get it right.

'The MC-8 taught me sight reading almost instantly. The way to learn about the micro composer is to get your favourite music in print form and bung it in. It is quite fast. I suppose to put in 32 bars would take me about three times as long as it would take me to play it on the piano. I would have to set pitch, step time and gate time – a couple of minutes. I don't look at the keyboard any more, I look at the score and my fingers find the right keys.

'I had no computer experience before I bought the MC-8. You don't need it, because the nice thing about the MC-8 is that the concept is so simple. It's no different from looking at black dots and numbers – in one way black dots are stranger. We see numbers every day.

'It expanded my musical horizons from day one. I wasn't able to read very well before and suddenly I was able to read because I was learning musical notation and the computer language simultaneously.

'Straight away I was able to write music on the machine without referring to conventional instruments. I bought the MC-8 just before Christmas and instead of sending out Christmas cards to all my friends I send them cassettes with little Christmas songs on. It pushed up my productivity.

'The MC-8 encourages you to get into deeper things. First of all, because the MC-8 has eight voices, once you've got the top line in, you want to do something with the other seven voices – just because they're there. So you start messing about. After a while you find out what is good and what isn't. I started putting classical scores into the machine – not because I wanted to do *Switched on Bach*, but just because there are certain pieces of classical music which I just enjoy listening to.

'I'd love to go completely digital. I'm toying with the idea of getting a Fairlight. But the top end of digital machines is not good enough. Their sampling rate just isn't fast enough.'

'For the first time I'm beginning to get the things I can imagine on
to vinyl and that's because of the Fairlight.'
Peter Gabriel.

'I suppose I've effectively had a year's worth of work on my Fairlight.
On the last album (Peter Gabriel III) we had just a few background
sounds from the Fairlight. There were also a few things we created
by strange processing rather than creating them on the Fairlight.
Some of the sounds people thought were the Fairlight weren't...they
were Prophets, voices or acoustic instruments, which we screwed up
in various ways. On this album (Peter Gabriel IV) we've used the
Fairlight a great deal.
'The Prophet was really my first introduction to programmable
instruments. Before that, Larry Fast had been doing virtually all the
synthesizer stuff . . . he's a master of sound and I learned a lot from
working with him.
'Electronic music excited me – Walter Carlos, Clockwork Orange –
all that stuff sounded fresh. But with computer music there was this
attraction of 'enlarging your palette of sounds.' The sort of things
that had not been available on analog were complex waveforms
which could include, for example, breath and finger noises which
provide sounds with distinctive personalities.
'I think finding new sounds is important: it's a bit like making a film
using well-known actors as against a new film with fresh faces.
There's some magic in the newness, it is a real force to be harnessed.
If you use the same old sound world, people are very familiar with
it and they're immediately going to hear all the cliches. The brain is
a device which assimilates selected bits of information and builds a
picture up. If you get a few building bricks with which you are
already familiar, you fill in the rest of the picture automatically. If
you are lucky enough to plug into an unusual way of using those
bricks, or find an unusual sound, then you have a new key to tap an
emotional response.
'Using orthodox sounds in unorthodox ways is also valuable –
anything that can defeat the tendency toward cliche is useful—unless
the cliche has a purpose.
'Years before I knew it was possible, I dreamed of an instrument like

the Fairlight....I remember interviews five or ten years ago, just fantasizing about an instrument that could play melodies and rhythms on any sound you chose. It was a writer's fantasy more than a player's, but I suppose I think of myself as a writer really. The whole thing about computers, is that the writer gains control over his music — for the first time, really.

'My Linn Drum has also altered the way I write. Part of the writing process on the last two albums has been that of rhythm first. Drum computers have offered me the ability to take my hands off the instrument and still have a great feel carry on. I like to find new rhythms, I think a lot of rock rhythms are getting boring. Half of the rhythm patterns on the new album are in a more traditional style with different emphases and the unusual patterns that were taken from a rhythm 'library' that I had built up with about 40 ideas. I may still use some of the remainder in the future.

'With the 'Biko' rhythm on the last album I was able to restrict myself to three chords, once I had it stored in the drum machine. The song wasn't a Linn creation, I started writing that in 1978, before I had a drum computer.

'The first drum machine I had was a very cheap thing made by an innovative company called Paia in America, it was a kit. That was introduced to me by Larry Fast — it cost around 70 quid. It was really useful, but on reflection the sounds were terrible — except for use as special effects.

'*The Rhythm of the Heat* on the new album actually began by fiddling around on the Fairlight. There was a rhythm on a loop — gur-doing, gur-doing — I fiddled with the loop length until I got it how I wanted it. With the Fairlight there's a shift towards making decisions with the vast range of source material, rather than hearing things in your head and going after them...it's play: generating stuff which stimulates enough to suggest a direction.

'Artificial intelligence is providing me with choices. Sometimes it will go the other way round and I will think of an arrangement, a colour to do a job, and create it. I've also found that as I learned to get more out of the Fairlight, I would have liked to have gone back to scratch with a lot of the tracks on the new album. The Fairlight works well as a decorator in places, but I think it works even better as a foundation builder. It can dictate the nature of the thing you are writing, as I allowed it to in *The Rhythm of the Heat*.

'I will probably spend a lot of time playing with the Fairlight now and the next album will probably make even more use of it. It will be play that will again trigger things that excite me and then I'll home in on those. Often my writing process has been to play with an idea continuously until I get bored, and then perhaps pick out two minutes of nuggets from a cassette of around 30 minutes – there's a lot of trial and error.

'There is another shift in emphasis the music computer is causing. It's removing the exclusivity, control and realization of ideas from the musician and passing it to the layman. I'm basically unqualified as a musician. I do read single lines of music, but not well. I have no technique really, no training, no formal understanding whatever – as is true for a lot of rock people. But now I am able to do things which before would have had to incorporate professional, specially-trained musicians. I'd maybe have to call in an arranger who perhaps would give me collaborating space, but it would be hard for me to say 'I want to do a strange squeak come slide that goes all the way from here to here' and have him know what I meant. Now I can fiddle with the controls until I have it. I may still want the performance of a live musician but at least he can listen to the outline of the idea.

'Both methods have strengths, but I've been told in the past that I can not do certain things, for one reason or another, so it is exciting to feel confined only by the limits of my imagination and not by the approaches, performances and styles of players and arrangers.

'When I first got to grips with the Fairlight I was over the moon. I was grabbing everyone around and saying listen to this!' I still get that feeling . . . there's so many veins to explore that you can still retain the basic enthusiasm of a kid. I feel both boredom and fatigue are seriously underrated creative forces and the Fairlight and Linn both invigorated my work — although I think there is always something I could find to turn me on. There is this feeling that there is another world of sound and music which is just around the corner.

'For the first time I'm beginning to get the things I can imagine on to vinyl and that's because of the Fairlight. On the last album (Gabriel III), I went for an unusual drum sound without cymbals and so on, and there was this landscape in which I felt encouraged to build unusual textures.

'At present the Linn does some things very much better than the Fairlight. The Fairlight's sampling of percussive sounds, specially the first part of the sound, hasn't got a wide-enough frequency range or a quick-enough response to get a really percussive edge to it. The

Linn composition process is terribly easy to work with and Fairlight are now putting something similar into their software. Another fantastic thing about this generation of instruments is that you don't have to get another instrument when something new comes along, you just get a new software disk although with the sampling improvement and updates they're actually going to have to send out new boards to be exchanged in the computer.

'Some of the old fashioned musical instrument companies think the musician is a thickie: they're making computer instruments in varnished wood cases and they don't do half the things they could. It's the Casios of this world who have got it right: they're going to give people the creative versatility. They haven't really produced the right instrument yet for musicians, but that Casio VL-Tone is amazing for the price and a hint of things to come.

'I would say the Prophet philosophy was good. It was both pre-programmed and yet you could press an edit button and you had all the power there: it allows for both ends. Phil Collins had a Prophet on his last album which was very successful but for all the time he was recording I understand he didn't realize you could alter the patches and edit. Now he's realized and it's a whole world opening up for him.

'I remember going round the Moog factory some time ago, looking at the Polymoogs: there were these three volume controls which controlled separate parts of the keyboard, and none of them went down to zero. Moog told me they had had to put a metal band in about two or three notches up because they were getting all these Polymoogs returned from shops with complaints that they wouldn't work. That's because they hadn't known to put these volumes as well as the master volumes up. By giving the musician that extra degree of control it was costing them a lot of money. That's why a lot of these manufacturers are frightened of allowing musicians to be intelligent. It's the double approach that you need: quick access to the juicy areas of sound to stage two with a wide range of programmable versatility.

'Real computer power encompasses a wide area: my knowledge of MCL (Fairlight's composing language) is minimal, I use MCL as a sequencer effectively. At present, what I'm doing is sampling sounds, controlling those samples, modifying and mixing them together.

'That's something else that's very interesting: you might start with the hit of a drum, and then add the sound of a guitar string to it.

There is that power: you can imagine it and you can get it.

'When you needed a rhythm in the old days you had to ask the drummer to play a suitable pattern. Good players do not always respond well to having their part written for them. Often they would create a better part than the composer, but sometimes this was at the expense of the originality of the composition. The composer can now score the part out of almost anything he can conceive. For instance, I was playing about on a Fairlight and we messed about speeding up the looping of a snare drum to such a point that we were getting to a single frequency and it sounded like an organ. So I started off with the drums and they got faster and faster and faster, and suddenly an enormous harmonic builds up from deep down which rises up and comes out like an organ. I was really turned on with that. Again it came out of play.

'My next project is to get to grips with MCL. There's enormous creativity possible in editing and updating – like computer mixing. Instead of having the strain of trying to remember a thousand different mixes, you can hold in memory whatever it is you first thought of and then update and improve on it.

'It is exactly that process that I used with cassettes in my writing. But it would take me an awful lot longer. The actual drudgery of going through all these tapes of shit to find the good parts was ridiculous. It is now short-circuited because I can create my starting sounds on the Fairlight and update it quickly.

'For me, the big buzz from the Fairlight in my first year of ownership is sampling and manipulating those sounds and also restructuring them – for example to get two or more sounds put together in different ways.

'Getting the right sample rate for a particular sound is always trial and error. You get a sound you want to put in and then you try it at one sample speed and then another. I record the sounds on a Nagra (a portable, professional tape recorder) first. Then sample them from tape.

'I found it quite hard learning the Fairlight from the manual, I had some people to help me and the 'Help' page in the software is very useful. When you're dealing with a particular problem on a particular page you can dial up help to get the answers which refer to that page.

'I've used one or two of the sounds provided with the Fairlight. There is an industrial saw which is on one of their sound effects disks: I used this on the new album, but I've reversed it and put a vibrato on it and it sounds a squeal.

'The only problem with music computers is the time it takes to get to grips with them, but I'm sure the machine's are going to get friendlier. The learning process has taken time. Going round recording lots of samples – from musicians, scrap yards, factories etc – was very time consuming. Quite a lot of the stuff we did was redundant. A lot of metal objects, when struck, sound like each other. For example the variation between the hitting and scraping of an exhaust pipe was far greater than hitting two different objects. Again it wasn't so much the range of input, it was the decision how best to use it.

'All sorts of natural sounds are useful once they're in the Fairlight. I like a lot of the percussive stuff and I think that's an area that I've enjoyed a lot and also I think I make judgements on the personality of the sound as it goes in – almost on an introvert/extrovert scale. I know that some will end up with a lot of vibrato, one might have a lot of attack, and it will be a bold extrovert sound. Another will be intentionally thin and flat.

'Long sounds, like running water, will only sound interesting when the software is better because there isn't enough sampling time yet – any sustained sound is difficult. Of course, there are various echoing devices which will extend things.

'I'm listening to sounds in a different way now knowing what I can do afterwards. I do find myself listening to sounds more carefully in day to day activities.

'There's tremendous control possible in playing back the sounds. One good idea is to adopt the pointillist technique Wendy Carlos and Larry Fast do in their analog synthesizer material. They often structure the variation that a real player provides into electronic music by painstakingly programming differences between one note in the sequence and the next. One way of doing that with the Fairlight is to apply all eight voices to producing the one sound but each with slightly different characteristics, e.g. attack, decay, vibrato. You have them all directed to the keyboard and get them in a sequence so that the first note to play is voice one, the second note is voice two and so on – so you always have this variation. With the MCL this focused on a monophonic line will bring it to life. With normal synths, so few people have got the time or the patience or the recording budget to do that.

Peter Gabriel. One of the world's most important songwriters, he draws new sounds and inspiration from the Fairlight, Linn and other computer musical instruments. He believes that computers offer composers new freedom to express themselves and will cause a shift of musical emphasis from the performer to the composer. (Picture by Robert Ellis, with thanks to Sounds *for its reproduction.)*

'Digital recording is another way in which computers are changing things for the musicians. Part of the recording of my new album was done digitally and mixed for the Compact Disk and other future digital systems. I know that with these systems there will be no generation loss between the mix and the final equipment that replays it. We compared a mix on a half-inch 30 i.p.s. tape, which is supposed to be state-of-the-art analog to a digital mix. We listened to them both without knowing which we were hearing and we preferred the digital mix. You hear a definite sound difference. The digital was significantly better and was obviously free of system noise.

'Some engineers argue that there is colouration of the sound with digital, from the way it processes the information, but I can't hear it – maybe we've all got too used to tape colour. People miss the hiss. Often you find when working with digital you switch the machine on and you can't hear anything so you crank the volume up and it suddenly blasts you.

'I would like to see more performance controls fitted to music computers. I think the more real-time performance controls the better. With the harmonium you had those swell flaps that could be operated with your knees and there is some experimentation now going on with breath-sensitive pipes as another control function – more physical interface is needed. I have talked to various people in the past who are interested in biofeedback about connecting humans directly to electronic instruments.

'Towards the end of my time with Genesis we performed *The Lamb Lies Down on Broadway* and I was trying to organize the opening of the show with all five of us connected to biofeedback devices in turn connected to synthesizers. They would read the drummer's heart beats, skin resistances and brainwave activity to get physical interface with sound. I think there is an area to be explored there. Again, the less abstractions you have, the more close you can get it to the source and the stronger the feedback relationship, the learning loop – although some of the brainwave outputs would contain uncontrollable elements.

'With the Fairlight, I've ended up tossing coins a lot. Selecting between options I've created. I want to by-pass my natural prejudices and abdicate responsibility when I feel equally drawn to two areas. So with this extra burden of responsibility I feel very happy to interface with chance. This brings in all sorts of philosophical arguments about chance. In some ways I'm a fatalist and I don't really believe in accidents, but I do think that when artists, or people, are really in tune with their work, they go with whatever is the direction of the flow at that time. It works. It often doesn't matter which way they turn, if they're hot, any direction will prove fruitful. 'I think the computer is going to force the musicians to come to terms with themselves. There will be more people with access to tools and I believe this will encourage artists to challenge themselves and dare to go into things they've been avoiding. The musician's interface with his art is going to be much more powerful − the psychological development of the artist is more likely to be revealed. He will still be able to evade reality by putting up an artifice, but much less easily.

'Of course, the whole process of recording information can change. A great deal of it will be done in the musician's home when the digital recording stuff becomes cheap enough. I will be able to send my tracks down the phone. If I want to work with a particular musician in a hurry I will call him up on the phone, transfer my stuff to him and he can add to it and send it back. Then I can mix what I want.

'In the past, there have been many attempts to relate colour and visual images to music. Now, for the first time it's really possible, using a computer to present representations of the wave shapes. There's only a degree of abstraction in choosing how to analyze the sound visually, and then the link is direct. I want to see colour coded to music. I want to see screens in studios so that you can see stuff before the point you're working at − perhaps 16 seconds ahead and you see what's on each track with the colour coding . The Fairlight shows sound waves in simulated 3D, so perhaps moving 3D image in colour would be ideal. It would be particularly useful for children and students trying to relate form, shape and structure of sound and music to its visual counterparts.

'There is a concrete visual dimension to music. It has always been there for the scientific analyst, but the public have never had access to it. As these applications are developed, we're going to see much more of this 3D full colour stuff. Analyzed scientific shapes might become boring after a while, but the marriage of music and visuals can go a long way. In film, for example, Kubrick can match music and visual images together for a complete emotional experience.

'It's another subject area, but this direct visual link might be really valuable in the learning process − learning about shapes, forms, etc.

The whole of education has been compartmentalized in the past but now there is going to be considerable cross referencing as in this example of art and music.

'There's always been a big barrier between science and art but it's mythical. It is going to be very hard to become an artist without understanding some scientific processes and vice versa. I'm having to learn elementary science to get the most from my computer music tools.

'There's a painter and a sculptor I'm working with at the moment. They're suggesting ideas to me about sound, I'm suggesting ideas to them about visual things. We will arrive at the point where a new medium of sound and vision is created without one being more important than the other. Some of the stars of this new medium will be from fine art, dance or ideas backgrounds – they'll be as much stars as rock musicians.

'Computers are changing all sorts of things. The whole interchange of information is altering as a result of the chip. For example, we created some sounds and stored them on a disk which has been passed on to other people. All of a sudden those sounds were cropping up on records, TV commercials, everywhere – I don't think copyright is worth losing any sleep over. People have made careers out of sounds generated by other people; that's happening all the time in pop or rock, and the equivalent has always happened in many art forms. I think that it is much better to aim for open access to all source material. It corresponds with the shift in emphasis from musician to composer – it is the decisions about how to use elements of other people's ideas that matter.

'I think the computer is going to cause a major change in society and that's really the most exciting thing about this whole thing. That's why it is so important for the labour movement not to take a Luddite view: they've got to harness the computer and use it lest it be used against them. Of course, there is this thing that power is access to information and I think free access should be a goal: forget copyright, forget home taping, forget all these things. Artists, musicians...we've just got to be better at it than everybody else, not desperately try to protect ourselves from plagiarism. No longer can we sunbathe in the backwaters, we'll have to get out in mid-stream and swim. I like that.

'I can't agree with attitudes I've heard coming out of the Musicians' Union regarding computers. One of the strengths in rock or pop is that it has such a vast turnover. It is a cruel business when things

don't sustain themselves one way or another; death, no income . . .
finish . . . go elsewhere . . . back to day jobs. That keeps you on the
edge; it's tough and I don't think you can protect or legislate against it.
Musicians shouldn't be afraid of computers, they should use them.
The same sort of process is going to affect a lot of people's lives and
I think we all need to become more versatile.

'Access to equipment is the answer: you've got physically handi-
capped people, mothers with young kids who are now performing
really useful jobs with computers in their homes. Before, they were
redundant. If they have access to tools they can now use their
intelligence. Get the computers out there!

'In the long term, much Marxist theory will become obsolete as the
exploitation of the masses becomes the exploitation of the micros.
Micro-controlled robots will run the factories and generate the
wealth with human labour shifting into social and service occupations.
The division will be between those with information — i.e. power —
and those without.

'But I'm afraid there are going to be violent Luddite groups — the
MU versus Linns and synthesizers is a microcosm of the reaction. A
Linn's bass drum sound is better than anything I could record from
a live drummer, but I don't think you can ever replace the human, a
drummer's personality and understanding of what is needed can't be
replaced. But of course anyone can become a rhythm maker now, I
think that's great. In the end it will be imagination that is the
deciding factor.'

Glossary of Jargon

Access
: Find. Access an item of information find an item of information.

ADC
: Analog to Digital Converter. A device which takes-in analog (electrical) information and converts it to numeric (digital) information. In music computers, the device which takes input from a keyboard (or other analog sound source) and converts it into information the computer can store.

Additive synthesis
: The process of building up a sound by adding harmonic waveshapes to a fundamental.

ADSR
: An acronym for Attack, Decay, Sustain and Release, referring to the dynamic characteristics common to all sounds. In an analog synthesizer the ADSR control provides control over these parameters and considerable sound modifying possibilities.

Alphanumeric
: Alphanumeric keyboard: a keyboard with letters and numbers as in a typewriter keyboard. Alphanumeric information: information consisting of letters and numbers.

Algorithm
: The various steps necessary to find the solution to a problem. A logical progression of procedures that will lead to the end result.

ALU
: Arithmetic and Logic Unit. Part of a central processor that actually executes the operations requested by an input command.

Analog
: An electronic signal whose waveform resembles that of the original signal. Analog synthesizers are those that produce sound by electronic means. Conversely, computers produce sound digitally, which is the numeric representation of sound. Computer music is not, and should not be called, electronic music.

ASCII
: The ASCII code is the 'American Standard

Code for Information Interchange.' This code has been developed to allow computers to communicate in a common language. Communication is often by telephone, computers connected via modems. The rate at which information passes is relatively slow.

Assembler language A language that is close to the original binary language of computers. The language includes symbolic machine language statements which relate directly to the instruction and data formats of the computer. Used by advanced programmers.

Assignable Capable of altered function. An 'assignable' control may have several functions under the control of software.

Audio-cassette interface A connection allowing ordinary cassette recorders to be connected to computers for the purpose of storing programs on cassette tapes.

Backup Copy. For safety reasons every computer program should be backed up so that if a program is lost during operation, or if a storage medium should become damaged, a safety copy, or backup is available. 'To backup' = to copy.

Bandwidth Frequency range. A hi-fi system can typically deliver sound between 20Hz and 20KHz (20 and 20,000 cycles). Many computer music systems can only produce sound in relatively narrow bandwidths – up to 10K for instance – but these can make acceptable sounds. The human auditory circuits classify everything above 5K as very high treble. When high-end is missing clarity and sparkle is the most noticeable lack.

BASIC 'Beginner's All-purpose Symbolic Instruction Code.' A high-level computer language developed in the fifties at Dartmouth College. BASIC is the language that most home computers work on. It is an ideal language for amateur programmers, but is too slow in operation for professional use.

Boot
To 'boot up' a disk. Jargon for inserting a disk, issuing the instruction to the computer to identify and initialize the disk and place it 'on line' for information storage and retrieval. A 'boot track' on a disk is a built-in program which carries out the above procedure.

Bubble memory
A non-volatile memory device which stores numeric information safely even when power is withdrawn. Information is stored as magnetic 'bubbles' on a sliver of synthetic garnet. Microscopic in size, the bubbles follow a path through a circuit and when stopped provide a pattern of 1 and 0 information which is a permanent memory. Expensive but excellent.

Bug
An error in a computer program. Software is such a complex science that many programs are sold to the public before all the errors (bugs) have been discovered. During use some of the errors show up and the manufacturers usually develop revised programs which are 'de-bugged' and supply them at nominal cost to existing users.

Byte
A byte is a 'phrase' made up of the smallest items in computer language — the 'bits.' Often 8-bits make a byte and that phrase can represent one character or two numerals.

C language
A high level programming language used by factory software writers. Soon to be used as the main language in a major dedicated music-computer.

Chip
Slang for microprocessor. Actually a very thin slice of semi-conductor material on which microscopic electronic components are photo-etched to make circuits. It becomes an 'integrated circuit' when connection tags and a plastic case are added. Complete microcomputers on chips are now possible, usually

	measuring only a quarter or an inch square.
Click-track	Once tempo is set for recording, a click track is placed on to one track of a multi-track tape machine. This track provides synchronization for later parts.
Come up	Jargon for powering up a computer.
Control voltage	The electrical signal which, in an analog synthesizer, specifies which frequency is played by the oscillators.
CPU	Central Processing Unit. The primary unit of a microcomputer that includes the circuits controlling the interpretation and execution of instructions.
CRT	Cathode Ray Tube. A television-type screen.
Cursor	The 'blinking dot' on a computer screen that shows the user where he is working.
DAC	Digital to Analog Converter. A device which converts digital information in computers into analog (electrical or physical) signals which an audio system can amplify.
Data	Information that defines a specific task. A computer program may be written to solve a particular type of problem but specific 'data' must be provided before an individual calculation can be computed.
Debug	To find the fault in a computer program. Only necessary when new programs are generated, not when programming musically. A debugger is a program within a program that automatically searches for illegal program entries and reveals them to the user.
Dedicated	As in dedicated music computer. A computer designed specifically for one task.
Dot-matrix	Dot-matrix printer. A computer printer that makes up letters and graphics by firing dots of ink at the paper. More versatile than typewriter-quality printers and good for printing music.
Dump	1) 'Off load': usually applied when a program is 'dumped,' or off-loaded to storage medium

	such as disk or cassette.
	2) A power dump, when all power is removed from the computer.
Digital	The binary code: the 01011001-style numeric language on which all computers are based. Refers to systems that are computer based. Digital sound—sound that is stored as numbers.
Disk drive	The mechanical system which spins a floppy disk at high speed and applies a magnetic head immediately above the surface of the disk for information access. In some computers the disk drives are built into the chassis, in others they are supplied as separate, free-standing-units connected by ribbon cable. A typical disk drive provides 150-300K of storage.
DMA	Direct Memory Access. A form of data transfer employed when it is vital that information should be stored and retrieved quickly from disk. In this system, data is transferred automatically after the CPU has initiated the transfer without requiring supervision, freeing the CPU for other tasks.
Eight(8)-bit	*See* Sixteen(16)-bit.
Envelope	The 'shape' of a sound, when displayed graphically; typically of an 'ADSR' pattern. A graph indicating the development of a sound.
Event-recorder	Used by some music-computer companies to describe a sequencer-type program. Notes, rests, and ties are all events in music and when a sequencer is described as an event recorder it usually means that the system will store information about which notes were played but will not store information about how they were played: key velocity, etc.
Fourier synthesis	The Fourier mathematical formula argues that any complex waveform may be resolved into a fundamental plus a set number of harmon-

ics. A formula widely used to allow computers to compute the gaps between information supplied about harmonic envelopes.

Floppy disks
A storage medium for computer information. Looks similar to flimsy disks used for promotions by the record industry but is protected in a paper sleeve. Disk spins at high speed inside paper sleeve when inserted in disk drive and the information, stored in 'tracks' on the disk, is read by a magnetic head that floats above the surface of the disk. An efficient, cost-effective method of information storage and retrieval.

Free-standing
Not part of a greater item of equipment.

Fundamental
In waveshaping, the root harmonic on which other harmonics are built.

Graphics display
A CRT screen built specifically for displaying graphics. Many ordinary computer screens do not have sufficiently high-resolution for high-quality graphics displays. Fairlight had to have a screen custom-built to allow its graphic displays of sound waves to be shown.

Go down
Letting the system 'go down.' Turning the thing off. Sole meaning in computer parlance.

Hard copy
Printout on good old-fashioned paper.

Hard disk
An advanced, large capacity, storage system for microcomputers. Only just available (for a few dedicated music-computers), hard disks operate like floppy disks, but store four or more times the amount of information.

Headroom
A term that has spilled over into music-computing from the recording industry. Headroom was the gap between the peak working level on tape and the point at which the sound might actually distort. In computer parlance 'having the headroom' means having sufficient spare computing power.

Hexadecimal
A code of counting in which 16 is used as the base. Used in low-level computer lan-

guages which are slow to write but very flexible.

High-level language
The language in which the end-user writes programs. These languages usually allow programming in English-type statements such as 'goto' or 'next' and are developed to allow users to consider the problems in hand rather than worrying about correct addressing of the microprocessor. Machine language is the final target language and is controlled by a structure of high-level language controlling intermediate languages. In effect this is a layered operation: the user says what he or she wants in plain terms, the high-level language translates that into compiler, the compiler issues instructions to assembler which generates machine code.

I/O device
See input/output device.

Illegal commands
An instruction the computer is unable to recognize.

Initialize
The start-up procedure for computer systems using peripheral units such as disk drives or printers. The initialization program sets up the starting condition.

Input/output device
Any device which allows the computer to communicate with the outside world, and vice versa. An alphanumeric keyboard is an I/O device, so is a CRT screen (when a light pen is added for input), a musical keyboard is often an input device and sometimes also an output device.

Instruction
A coded program step that tells the computer what to do next.

Integrated circuit
IC. A group of circuits formed at the same time which are interconnected and capable of performing a complete function. The IC is usually mounted in a plastic package and connecting pins protrude from two sides rather like legs.

Interface
Matching connection. For a computer to

182

	interface with a synthesizer a suitable interface (matching connection) must be made.
Keys-down	Keys-down information. Information from musical-keyboard keys: how hard the key was played, how fast it was pushed down, how long was it held down etc. This is the 'keys-down' information that a high-quality music computer system should be able to read from the musical keyboard. This information is stored and reproduced to control replay of the sounds. It may be edited by the user.
Keystroke	One 'press' of a key on an alphanumeric keyboard.
LCD	Liquid-Crystal Diode. A display system often found in inexpensive electronic items. Made by sandwiching liquid-crystal and electrodes between two sheets of glass. Current causes the liquid to change its light-trapping properties so forming letters or numbers.
Light pen	A clever, high-speed pen-shaped device which, when held against a CRT, can issue instructions for program or graphics purposes. The pen usually doesn't admit light, a photo-sensitive cell in the pen reacts to light from the screen. Placing the pen over the relevant command shown on a screen will cause that command to be carried out. Simple versions can be seen reading bar codes at supermarket check-outs. Casio apply a similar system for entering music from bar codes into their small microprocessor keyboards.
Load	To place the program into the computer's 'live' RAM memory — usually loading is done from a storage device such as cassette or disk.
Lockout	A situation during computer operation when the arithmetic and logic units both try to access the CPU at the same time — usually the result of illegal commands in an

unfriendly program. The computer just ceases to work. Only solution is to turn the damn thing off and start again – losing the work in hand.

Low-pass filter — Also high-pass filter. Filters which allow certain frequencies to pass, but 'cutoff' unwanted frequencies. Used in music computers to reduce unnecessary frequency analysis.

LSI — Large Scale Integration. The state of the art before the VLSI. Refers to a component density of more than 100 per chip.

Machine language — Binary language, the language of 0 and 1 that all computers finally work on.

Mainframe — Mainframe refers to the basic or main part of the computer, the CPU. In everyday use mainframe computer refers to the large, ultra-powerful computers operated by governments and multi-national corporations in which the 'main' element in the name distinguishes the unit from smaller satellite terminals which may be able to interface with it.

Menu-driven — A software-design style in which the program offers the user a 'menu' of choices whenever a decision has to be made. Rapidly gaining in popularity, menu-driven programs are easy to use and reduce the demands on the end user to a minimum.

Microcomputer — A small computer system, usually based on one or two microprocessors, which sells for a few hundred dollars or pounds. Typical units use domestic television screens for display, interface with domestic cassette recorders for ROM and have no hard printout facility built-in.

Microprocessor — The CPU (Central processing unit) of a computer. Built in layers on a microscopic chip of silicon.

Modem — A MODulation/DEModulation device that

allows computers to connect to telephone lines. Using a Modem to hook into the telephone lines allows computers in remote locations to interchange information using the ASCII code.

Monophonic One note. A monophonic system can play only one note at one time.

Multiplexer A device that takes input from several sources and delivers them in one high-speed stream of information.

Music Concrète The pioneering style of electronic music popular in the 1950s and 1960s which, to some extent, has got synthesized and computer music a bad name.

Nanosecond Particle of time equal to one billionth of a second (UK equivalent is one thousand, millionth of a second).

Nest(ed) A program within a program. Nested menus are menus that offer decision choices subsequent to original menu choice.

Off-load To store program on magnetic storage device such as cassette or disk.

On-line 1) Available. Being 'on line' means that a piece of information, a program or a computer peripheral is ready to be used.
2) Communicating.

Operating system The basic programs that cause the computer to operate before specific function programs are loaded.

Overlay A system of software design which allows long programs to be written and stored on disk ready to be called when required. During operation the part of the program currently in RAM will automatically call the next part of the program out of ROM which will load into RAM 'overlaying' and erasing the earlier program.

Parameter A variable; a measurement.

Peripheral A computer peripheral is a unit that is separate to the main computer — a printer, a disk drive, a musical keyboard.

Port	A socket, usually built into the computer, which allows information to pass in and out.
Polyphony	The ability to sound more than one note at the same time. 8-voice polyphony the ability to sound eight separate notes at once.
Program	Never programme. A list of instructions telling a computer precisely what to do. In musical applications a program might be the order of musical events as entered by a musician into a computer-based instrument.
Quantization	Quantization noise/quantization error. The noise which occurs in digital sound reproduction when numerical expressions of sound are rounded off to their nearest numerical equivalent. Every measurement may be expressed in infinite terms, but when measurement is rounded off for the purposes of finite computation, small errors occur and, in sound reproduction, cause background noise. In musical applications, the more power the computer has the greater degree of measurement accuracy is possible, thus the lower the level of background noise. A problem that has been largely overcome.
RAM	Random Access Memory. The operating part of a computer's memory. The user can access any part of this memory at random and order it to perform computations. RAM is the main measurement of computer power. Home computers currently offer between 1K and 128K RAM, although some home/business machines are capable of offering up to 900K RAM. Music computers rise to 256K RAM and above.
Real-time	Live: happening now. When you play a piano you are playing in real-time. When you program a computer to play a piano part you are programming in real-time but, as a whole, the piece of music has been created out of

real-time. When the computer plays the program it is playing non-real-time music.

Reset-switch
A switch found on most microcomputers which completely wipes all RAM and resets the computer to an 'empty' mode.

ROM
Read Only Memory. A non-volatile (permanent) memory system which can only be 'read from' in a certain sequence. Information stored in the memory cannot be accessed at random, but must be loaded into RAM where it may be accessed. ROM is used for the permanent and semi-permanent storage of information and typical ROM mediums include ROM chips (on which a program is written by the factory), floppy disks, hard disks and cassette tapes.

Sampling Rate
In musical applications, the rate at which a computer measures sound. External sound is fed to a music computer, e.g. the Fairlight, via an analog to digital converter. Within this device the sound wave is measured a fixed number of times per second. The frequency at which the sound is measured is called the sampling rate and the higher the rate, the more accurate the sample. For professional fidelity, the sampling rates chosen by the recording industry are between 40,000 and 50,000 times per second.

Semiconductor
The item at the heart of the computer. A material with an electrical conductivity somewhere between a good conductor (metal) and a poor conductor (insulating material.) Its conductivity increases as its temperature rises. As a device, a semiconductor is made from silicon, germanium or similar material and its basic function in computer applications is to represent 'on' or 'off': expressed another way, 1 or 0.

Sequencer
A microprocessor device for remembering control information. In the past sequencers

have been used to control analog synthesizers, but now most computer-based instruments have built-in sequencers which act like tape recorders. They record all of the information from a series of notes and will replay those notes on demand. Many allow 'overdubbing.'

Silicon
One of the earth's most common materials (covering our beaches), silicon has proved to be one of the most important materials ever applied in technology. A perfect semi-conductor and the material from which most microprocessors are constructed.

Sixteen(16)-bit
The 'bit' size in computer measurement parlance refers to the number of bits that can move through a computer at once – the width of information that can be handled. The wider the path, the more information can pass through at one time. Many TV games operate quite successfully on a 4-bit system, standard home computers are currently 8-bit and the new generation of microcomputers use 16-bit – e.g. the IBM personal and the Radio Shack Model 16.

Some computer designs use 16-bit systems in one part of the information path and 8-bit in others. Microprocessors themselves are designed as 8-bit or 16-bit units. At the beginning of 1981 several US corporations announced the development of 32-bit microprocessors and although there are, as yet, no domestic systems or software programs available using this technology, the 32-bit system will produce a microcomputer with power equivalent to some of the mainframe computers. Most music computers are currently using 8-bit technology.

Soft
Soft-instrument. An increasing number of musical instruments are now soft. The phrase means that the instrument is computer-based

	and performs according to software instructions. Modification in the software results in a change in the instruments performance. Fully soft instruments are not yet with us; all current music computers require some special hardware to carry out musical functions. This special hardware limits the adaptability of the instruments. It is likely that the first really soft instruments will appear within five years.
Software	A collective name for all computer programs. Instructions for the computer are always soft, the mechanical and electrical elements of the computer are hardware.
Software gap	A gap that is opening between the capabilities of hardware and the people who write programs to control it. Computer development is following an exponential curve and artificial intelligence capability is increasing by compound leaps each year. Programmers are struggling to write programs that make efficient use of power now available.
Solid-state	Any electrical circuit built without electromechanical parts such as tubes (valves). Transistor circuitry.
Speech-analyzer	A system that can recognize spoken words and transform them to computer commands. Under heavy research, but proving difficult to perfect. Ask a computer to differentiate between 'I saw' and 'eyesore.' Speech recognition is one of the major goals of the Japanese drive to develop the '5th Generation' of computers, but successful recognition systems capable of fully understanding speech might not be available for ten years.
String	A string of numbers or letters grouped together: usually in a computer program.
Stripe card reader	A device that decodes information contained in a strip of magnetic tape usually embedded in a plastic card. As used in Yamaha digital instruments and others.

Subroutine	A secondary part of a computer program which is called up during program operation to carry out a specific task.
Tracks	A term sometimes used by companies producing soft instruments to describe a multiple sequencer. In suggesting that a digital sequencer has 16-tracks, the manufacturers are comparing the system to 16-track analog tape recorders to help users visualize the facility. Often the facility isn't identical as tracks placed on top of tracks can't be accessed separately for subsequent editing or mixing.
Trigger	To trigger: to set-off, to start. A trigger into an analog input causes the relevant note to sound.
User-friendly	Usually applied to program design. A user-friendly program or system is one that makes operation easy for unskilled operators.
User language	The language in which the user communicates with the computer – often bad!
Utilities	Basic programs in a computer system such as DOS (disk operating systems) and languages.
VDU	Visual Display Unit. VDUs are intended for business use and display 80 characters horizontally against the more normal 40 characters found on micro-computer screens.
Wave	As in sound wave. The shape of the graph (wave-like) that represents the frequency of a sound.
Waveform memory	A computer memory device, either RAM or ROM, which holds all of the information pertaining to a waveform.
Waveform table	A method of arranging information about a waveform that sets it out as a table in computer memory allowing the user rapid access to any part of the information.
Write	To copy. To write to disk means to copy the information on to a disk for storage purposes.

Index

See also Glossary of Jargon

Adaptive Systems Inc. 101
    Synthia 101, 102
AFM (American Federation of Musicians) 76
ALF music system 26, 27, 28
alphaSyntauri system *see* Syntauri
Apple/Apple II computer 22, 26, 27, 29, 31,
    33, 35, 48, 61, 62, 64, 69, 70, 71, 102
Apple soft language 31
BASIC programming language 24, 25, 157
BBC Radiophonic Workshop 155
Boody, Charles 69
British Musicians' Union, Central London
    branch 75, 76, 174
Bubble memory 15, 79, 80, 110
Cann, Warren 7, 86, 147−154, 161
Carlos, Wendy 165, 170
Casio 21, 124
    Casiotone CT-401 54
    VL-Tone 21, 52, 169
CBS
    DISComputer 47
    Rhodes Chroma synthesizer 102
Chamberlin, Hal 28, 44
Commodore PET computer 48, 61
Converter
    analog to digital 11, 43, 46, 63, 107, 124,
      125, 143
    digital to analog 43, 107, 143
CPU (central processing unit) 15, 109, 129
    6800 134
    6809 134
Crumar
    GDS (General Development System)
      143, 144
    Synergy digital synthesizer 108, 109
Depeche Mode 90
Digital Keyboards, Inc.
    Synergy digital synthesizer 108, 109
Digital recorders/recording 41, 42, 46, 98,
    107, 172
Dolby, Ray 41
Echo devices, analog 38
Electronics and Music Maker 24
Electrophon Company 21
Emerson, Keith 7
EMS VCS3 155
    256 155
E-mu Systems, Inc. 15
    Audity 105
    Emulator 15, 105−108

European Broadcasting Union 43
Eventide Real Time Audio Spectrum
    analyzer 48
Fairlight CMI (computer musical
    instrument) 9, 28, 46, 77, 88, 104,
    126−146, 154, 159, 162, 166, 167, 169,
    171, 172
Fast, Larry 165, 166, 170
Fourier additive harmonic synthesis 28, 31,
    136, 138, 145
Furse, Tony 127, 128
Gabriel III 165
Gabriel IV 165
Gabriel, Peter 7, 75, 165−175
Gnat synthesizer 24
Helden 161, 162, 163
Hexadecimal code 28
Hodgson, Brian 155
Human League, the 7, 13, 46, 49, 75, 90
IBM personal computers 62
Information transmission 45
Input methods 14, 55
    alphanumeric 14, 21, 55, 66, 129, 131,
      137, 143, 159
    calculator 111, 116, 129
    musical 14, 55, 137
    voice 14
Jarre, Jean-Michel 7, 9
Josephson junction, the 10
Kakehashi, Ikataro 11, 84
Kellner, Charles 70
Keyboard, dynamic 108
Kinetic Sound Corporation
    Prism digital synthesizer 109, 110, 111,
      112
Kraftwerk 7, 18, 90
Kuhn, Wolgand 71
Landscape 7, 116
Language, computer/programming
    Applesoft 31
    assembler 125, 128
    BASIC 24, 25, 157
    Fairlight MCL 130, 137−141, 157, 168,
      169, 170
    FORTH 25
    Pascal 25
    user 125
Lewis, John 154−160
Linn Electronics Corporation 75
    LM-1 drum computer 75

Linn Drum, the 49, 76, 77, 78, 80, 81,
    142, 148, 152, 159, 161, 175
Linn, Roger 153
Lockout 66
Lorton, Paul 71
McCartney, Paul 47
McClevyier dedicated instrument 138, 143
Machine code 24, 25
Marsh, Ian Craig 91
Mattel 84
    Synsonics drum machine 84—88
Maydew, Peter 24
MDP Polysequencer 121
Metatrack software package 37
Moog, Robert 11, 131
MTU Instrument synthesis package 28
Musical Applications of Microprocessors 28,
    44
Musicomp program 26, 63—66
Neve Electronics 47, 48
    DSP (fully-digital recording studio
        console) 47, 48
Nunnery, Brian 163
Oberheim 80
    DMX drum computer 80, 81, 121
    DSX keyboard sequencer 121
Orchestral Manoeuvres in the Dark 7, 75, 90
PACE 92, 93
    DM series multi-track console 92
Passport Designs 31, 35, 68
    Soundchaser system 29, 31, 32—34, 68,
        70
        analog 31, 32, 69
        digital 29, 32, 69
Philips 56, 58
    G7000 Videopac computer 56, 57, 61, 67
PPG 112, 113, 144
    Wave 2.2 polyphonic keyboard
        synthesizer 112, 113
    Waveterm 143—145
Qasar M8 127, 128
Quad-8 desk 39
Radio Shack TRS-80 61
Rance, Steve 163
Roland Corporation 11
    Bass Line TB-303 122
    Boss Doctor rhythm unit 73
    CPE-800 Compu-Editor 40, 93
    Jupiter-8 98
    MC-4/MC-8 MicroComposers 13, 49,
        74, 98, 116—120, 161, 163, 165
    TR 77 rhythm unit 147, 149
    TR 78 rhythm unit 149, 150
    TR-606 drum machine 82
    TR-808 rhythm composer 83

Rosum, Dave 105
Rushent, Martin 11, 46, 49
Ryrie, Kim 127, 131, 142, 146
Sampling rate, sound 42, 43, 107, 132, 169
Sequencers/sequencer capacity 18, 24, 25,
    32, 35, 37, 49, 98, 107, 109, 122, 138, 151,
    152, 159
Sequential Circuits 90, 95—98
    Prophet 5/10 synthesizers 90, 94—98,
        102
Sharp MZ-80K home computer 25, 61
Sinclair ZX81 personal computer 22, 23, 24,
    61, 95
Software 29
    copyright problems 15
    'gap' 62, 83, 125
    menu-driven 26, 30, 63, 65, 68, 126,
        130, 139
Sony DMU-1520 digital preview unit 47
    PCM digital audio processor 47
Star Instruments Inc.
    Synare MP (mallet percussion) 87, 88
Syntauri Corporation 29, 70
    alphaSyntauri system 35—37, 63, 70, 71
Synthesizers see also under names and makers
    analog 11, 14, 22, 28, 90, 98, 102, 105,
        139
    digital 22, 62, 87, 98, 109
Tangerine Dream 7, 18
Tape recorders, 24-track, problems with 38
Teac 8-track 41
Texas Instruments 20, 79
    TI-499/A home computer 20, 67
Toto 7
Tug of War 47
Ultravox 7, 75, 147—154, 161
Vogel, Peter 127
Voorhouse, David 157
Wasp synthesizer 24
Waveform generation 137
Who's Next 98
Who, the 98
Wonder, Stevie 7
Yamaha 54, 55, 94, 99, 100, 104, 161
    GS1/GS2 digital performance-oriented
        instruments 99
    HandySound HS-500 54, 55
Young, Neil 7
Zimmer, Hans 118, 161—164
ZX81 see Sinclair

192